Horse Care For The Total Beginner

Jevon .E Hanna

Introduction

This is a comprehensive guide that provides essential information for individuals who are new to horse ownership or considering bringing a horse into their lives.

This guide covers a wide range of topics, from setting realistic expectations to understanding the basic needs of horses and preparing for their care.

The guide starts by emphasizing the importance of setting expectations when it comes to horse ownership. It acknowledges that horses are magnificent animals but also discusses the responsibilities and commitment required. It encourages readers to familiarize themselves with horses, their behavior, and their needs before making a decision to become a horse owner.

One of the key aspects of responsible horse ownership discussed in the guide is understanding what horses require from their owners. This includes essential elements like providing clean water, ensuring a proper diet that includes roughage and grain, and addressing their medical and farrier needs. The guide stresses the importance of regular attention and care to maintain the horse's health and well-being.

Choosing the right home for a horse is another critical topic covered in the guide. It explores the ideal horse habitat and offers insights into whether to keep a horse at home or board it. It provides readers with important questions to consider when making this decision, helping them choose the most suitable living arrangement for their horse.

Preparing to care for a horse is a significant step in horse ownership, and the guide offers valuable advice on this front. It outlines the essential items and facilities needed before a horse arrives, ensuring that readers are well-prepared to meet their horse's needs. Additionally, it discusses the process of moving a horse into a new space and the importance of establishing a routine for both the horse and the owner.

Overall, this book is a comprehensive and informative resource that covers the fundamental aspects of horse ownership. It serves as a valuable guide for individuals who are new to the world of horses, helping them make informed decisions and providing practical advice for the care and well-being of these magnificent animals. Whether someone is considering horse ownership or has recently become a horse owner, this guide equips them with the knowledge and understanding necessary to provide responsible and compassionate care for their equine companions.

Contents

SECTION 1: SETTING EXPECTATIONS

For those who are new to horse ownership, there may have been several terms in the introduction that were unfamiliar, or raised questions. How many types of hay are there? What do you mean by "parasite control?" Does having horses mean I need to exterminate every opossum I find?

Horse care can be very complicated, especially when you're diving into the concept for the first time. Much like people, different horses need different types of care. There is no "one-size-fits-all" universal standard for horse care. Over time, you may need to tinker with your program to ensure that the needs of your horse are being met. Things like overall health, the quality and quantity of natural forage, and the level of activity your horse performs on a daily basis can require you to rethink everything, from the type of feed you use to how much bedding you put in your horse's stall.

External factors can impact your horse care regimen as well. You'll find yourself paying close attention to the weather forecast, for example. Horses generally don't mind getting wet, but lightning and metal horse shoes don't mix well. Further, too much mud can lead to hoof issues. When it's hot, your horse might be at a greater risk for overheating and potential colic, and when the temperatures plummet, water buckets freeze and your equine buddy may need extra nutrition to help him cope with the cold.

It may seem a bit obvious, but in order to really appreciate what goes into horse care, you need to understand a thing or two about horses. Anyone who has enjoyed the companionship of a horse could write a book called "Everything I Know about Horses," and no two books would be identical. In fact, each book would contain so many contradictions, exceptions, footnotes, and addendums that no one could possibly get through it without a massive headache.

So instead, this section is going to overview the partnership we enjoy with horses in a manner that highlights some of the most important things about horse care that aren't as patently obvious as others. There are many assumptions and generalizations about horses in the world that simply aren't true or are even potentially dangerous when applied universally. In this section, I'll endeavor to reveal some common misconceptions and "I didn't know that" moments I've shared with many first-time owners and caretakers. While we'll examine some of the very basics, I want to empower readers to understand their individual horse and not just the general concept of "a horse." What *your* horse needs may be very different from what your best friend's horse needs.

It's my opinion-- and that of many professionals in the equine world-- that the more you know the beast, the more prepared you are to realize you don't know everything about them. As paradoxical as that sounds, you should start to understand what that statement means as you read on.

In the following chapters, we'll look at the basics of what makes horses tick and how our relationship with them works. While I wish there were a universal handbook, I think the only generalization we can make about horses is "all horses are unique." As you gain more experience with them, you'll understand exactly how true that statement is.

Chapter 1: Familiarizing Yourself with Horses

When you stop and think about it, it's really a bad idea to tangle with horses. Horses are large, quadrupedal prey animals. They're much larger than we are, both in height and weight. They're very muscular and, when motivated, incredibly fast, but they're just as prepared for fight as they are for flight. Their hooves are quite dense, and any of the four can strike out and kick to keep threats at bay. They have large teeth that continually grind the tough fibers of hay, grass, and grain to a digestible pulp. If the horse feels the need to protect itself, those same teeth can gnash through flesh very easily. Horses are big, fast, and dangerous, and it's important to keep this in mind at all times.

Horses are also among the most sensitive and empathetic animals humans have domesticated. As prey animals, they're naturally tuned in to their surroundings at all times. Their wide set eyes pick up all the motion around them, and their large ears swivel around to catch every nuance of sound in a 360-degree radius. Your horse will grow to understand patterns in how you move, how you speak, and how you interact with them. The short, hard strokes of the curry comb on their backs during a regular grooming session will tell them all about the bad day you had. The way your voice cracks when you call their name will expose how sad you've been feeling. Your super-relaxed demeanor will clue them in when you're having a good day. You can't keep secrets from a horse.

Likewise, as many wise horse experts have intoned, "horses don't lie." They have bad moods. Sometimes they don't feel good. Sometimes they flat out don't want to do whatever it is that you, as the human, have decided you need to be doing right now. Even more often, they simply don't understand what the human is asking of them.

Imagine, if you will, that you're hanging out in your bedroom. All of a sudden, someone walks in, makes you turn off your music and get out of bed. You have to put down the snack you were enjoying. They tie you up in the hallway, throw a backpack on you, and make you go for a hike.

Some of you might think, "Are you kidding? I love hikes! Let's do this!" Others are thinking, "Drop my snack and get out of bed? I don't think so!" Horses have the same variety of attitudes as we do. Some really enjoy working, and others need a little coaxing to get them prepared for the task ahead of them. Just as some mornings you wake up on the wrong side of the bed, so can your horse. They are not machines. They have bad days too. They are living beings who are doing the best they can with what they've got, just like you and me.

Just like people, horses also come in different shapes and sizes. The unit of measurement used to indicate how tall a horse is is called a "hand." A hand equals four inches. According to horse folklore, four inches is approximately the width of a man's hand from thumb to the outside of the pinkie finger. In the days before standard measurements, people would quite literally measure horses with their hands. Despite the development of more accurate measurements, the tradition of using the term "hands" when describing a horse's height remains. Therefore, if someone says a horse is 15 hands high, the horse is 60 inches tall.

Bear in mind, horses aren't measured from the ground to the top of their head. Any horse can raise or lower his head, which would change their measurements every time they bent down to graze. The top of their hip isn't used either since building muscle can cause a horse's hindquarters to grow in size. Instead, a horse's height is measured from the ground to the top of their withers. The withers are the spot where a horse's neck meets its back. For most horses, this is the tallest point of their body at all given times. There are exceptions, as some breeds tend to have hindquarters that tower above their withers, and spinal conditions such as lordosis can create a rather twisted version of a sway-backed horse. The distance from the withers to the ground very rarely changes, even as muscles grow or deteriorate, which is why this is used as the point of measurement for all horses' height.

To be considered a horse, the equine must measure over 14.2 hands (58 inches or 1.47 meters). Anything under this height is considered a pony. You may hear owners of giant 18 hand horses referring to their beasts as "my pony," but bear in mind this is more of a colloquial term of endearment, kind of like calling your grown cat a kitty.

In fact, there are many terms that horse people use to identify their beast. A mare is an adult female horse. A female horse under the age of four years is referred to as a filly. A male horse under the age of four years is a colt. An intact adult male horse is a stallion, while an adult male horse who has been castrated is a gelding. All of these terms may have different colloquial definitions, which muddies the water of understanding. For example, a mare with a feisty personality may be known to her humans as a "filly" for her entire life, though that's not technically accurate. This is similar to a parent calling her adult daughter "my little girl" despite her advanced age.

There are approximately 400 different horse breeds in the world today, though equine geneticists and breeders will argue the exact number eternally. Nearly every horse breed was created by crossing various bloodlines, which begs the question: "What was the original horse?" Thoroughbreds, for example, are alleged to have descended from three Foundation Arabian sires. The American Mustang tracks its bloodlines to the runaway horses of Spanish explorers. The American Quarter Horse is the result of crossing the horses of Spanish settlers with those of the English settlers. The Morgan horse breed is descended from a single stallion named Figure, who's own pedigree included a dash of Arabian, a sprinkle of Thoroughbred, and more than a little Welsh Cob, according to popular consensus.

Today, breeds are frequently evolving. The Georgian Grand, for example, is a rather recently acknowledged breed achieved by pairing a Friesian horse with an American Saddlebred. Another more modern breed is the American Sugarbush Harlequin Draft Horse, which was very carefully and deliberately bred from a particular Percheron bloodline paired with warmblood/Appaloosa crosses.

While some breed purists refuse to acknowledge some of the more modern breeds, or prefer to call them "crosses," there's no denying that certain breed attributes can contribute to the overall care needs of a particular horse. For example, Thoroughbreds can be what we call "hard keepers," in that they will lose weight whenever they're stressed, cold, or bored. Miniature ponies can be at high risk for medical conditions that come about from overfeeding. Appaloosas often have vision issues, and Quarter Horses from particular bloodlines can inherit genetic muscular problems, including HYPP, which can cause tremors and paralysis.

Additionally, some horses are better at certain jobs than others due to their breeding and conformation. Thoroughbreds that are bred for racing tend to be tall, lean, bold, and athletic. This makes them ideal for speed-based competition throughout their lives, whether that means pole bending or three-day eventing. Draft horses have the size and musculature to pull heavy loads, which makes them invaluable for pulling carriages or farm work.

Then there are gaited horses. Nearly every horse can walk, trot, and canter, which are the three main gaits of the typical riding horse. Some horses have extra manners of movement. The Paso Fino has quick-stepping gaits that make it appear to glide. Icelandic horses, though small in stature, seem to soar across the ground when they tolt. Standardbreds can pace very quickly on the racetrack, allowing them to cover a full mile in less than two minutes. Tennessee Walkers, Saddlebreds, and Missouri Fox Trotters are all examples of horses who have their own unique set of gaits.

So how do all of these differences translate to their care? To begin with, the amount of living space required. Not only will a bigger horse need a taller roof over its head, but it will need a larger space to stretch its legs as well. A horse bred to be very active will likely be less content with roaming around a field or standing in a stall and will need plenty of exercise. Gaited horses may require special shoes or hoof care to accommodate the different wear patterns they have from moving in a unique way. Some horses will need a lot of food to match their genetically predisposed metabolism while others are what we call "air ferns," meaning it seems as though they could gain weight just by breathing.

I have personally enjoyed the companionship of two very tall, very lean Thoroughbred geldings, a pregnant pony mare of unknown origins, a Quarter Horse mare with impeccable breeding, an aged Appaloosa gelding, and a very expressive Tennessee Walking Horse gelding. If I listed the care instructions for each one, you might think I was talking about six different species, rather than six wonderful horses. I have cared for horses who have multiple pages of care instructions just to get that single horse through the day. Some of this is based on owner preference and the job the horse is currently doing, but a great deal of their needs are determined by health, genetics, weather, and activity level, just like any other living creature.

Therefore, it is the responsibility of each horse owner to understand their horse on a nearly cellular level. There's a popular saying: "You don't ride bloodlines." You do, however, need to care for your horse based on its size, shape, breed, and even bloodlines.

The topic of various breeds and breeding is absolutely fascinating, and I recommend taking some time to do some research on the topic, especially if you're shopping for a horse that can do a very particular job. There are several links in the "Resources" section that can guide you to further information on this topic, so take some time to really explore the widely diverse world of *Equus caballus*.

Knowing more about horses can help you appreciate their behavior, moods, and care needs on a deeper level. As a horse owner, you'll quickly realize that you can never learn too much about these amazing animals and their quirks.

Chapter 2: The Many Considerations of Horse Ownership

Every day of horse ownership is new and different. One day, your horse might be super cuddly and almost make itself a nuisance begging for attention. The next day, it might be content with food, water, and being left alone. Living with a horse is like living with another human, in the way that you don't know what you're in for when you wake up in the morning. You just have to find a way to coexist.

It may sound like having a horse in your life is incredibly difficult physically, emotionally, and monetarily, but there are plenty of benefits to sharing your life with your horse.

Granted, most people no longer require horses for transportation, though there are still plenty of areas in which horses, mules, and donkeys are still very much valued for their ability to pull a cart, haul a rider around, or carry a heavy load. In many areas, horses provide vital contributions to agriculture by pulling plows in territories difficult for machines to navigate, or by dragging wagons for long distances. Horses are able to carry up to 20% of their body weight on their back. A horse can also pull up to 10% of its body weight in dead weight, though when wheels are added, a horse can pull up to 1.5 times its own body weight. A pair or a team of horses can pull tremendous loads reaching up to thousands of pounds. Horses are strong, nimble, sure-footed, and can navigate steep, muddy, and rocky terrain with admirable speed and endurance.

All of these qualities-- and more-- are what make riding, driving, and in-hand interacting with horses so delightful. There are many different disciplines, or styles, of riding which open the door to many ways in which you can work with your horse. Some people choose to study one particular discipline for their entire equine career, while others (myself included) prefer to explore as many as possible.

Riding, driving, and showmanship don't have to be all about horse shows and competition, either. There are plenty of equestrians who enjoy trail riding in their spare time, or practice dressage just for fun. One of the most common misconceptions about being an equestrian is that you need to spend loads of money to trailer your horse around to various big-name competitions to win points and prizes. Sure, horse shows can be a lot of fun, but they can also be very stressful for you and your horse. Once you've taken lessons for a while and have established a solid foundation in the discipline of your choice, you may wish to talk to your instructor about showing. But in the meantime, as long as you and your horse are having a good time, you don't need to have serious competitions or even a long term goal in mind.

Therefore, while some equestrians would say that the primary benefit of their horse is its ability to help them get work done, others would say the best thing about their horse is the fun they have together.

Furthermore, horses can be great companions. Their highly-tuned instincts make them incredibly perceptive of the nuances in your behaviors and moods. Nearly every horse owner has lost count of how many times they've broken down and cried on their horse's shoulder, or treated their horse like a therapist and told them absolutely everything that's going on in their life and in their heart. They are very good listeners and can usually be encouraged to listen to you as long as you need them to. However, you might just have to bribe them a little with scritchy-scratches on their favorite itchy spot, or a handful of treats.

Author's Anecdote: Old Mare's Tales about Mean Horses

We've all heard the old tales about some distant relative or friend's horse who was "nasty as could be" or "bit everyone he ever met", but that's actually pretty uncommon in the horse world. Yes, there are mean horses, but in many cases, their attitudes correlate to poor treatment, lack of training, or physical pain.

After nearly a decade in horse rescue, I have only ever encountered one horse who was "nasty as could be". She was a gorgeous little filly who had been surrendered by her breeder after being weaned because she kicked him with enough ferocity to break his leg. We worked with her slowly, grooming her, teaching her to lead, and growing her accustomed to having people near her. She was very smart and learned quickly, but her temper would come out of nowhere.

Horses typically prefer "flight" over "fight" and provide many visual cues with their body language to indicate when they're upset. They'll pin their ears, raise their head, swish their tail, bare their teeth, or tuck their hindquarters to indicate they're upset. This particular horse did none of these, which is how she ended up sending several seasoned equine professionals to the emergency room.

A thorough medical exam uncovered evidence of traumatic brain injury. Whether she experienced an accident careening around as a baby, or in the womb, we'll never know. But knowing that there was a physical cause for her attitude helped us adjust our care routine to help her become more comfortable, and kept us safer.

While horses can have bad days and foul moods, if you notice an abrupt or lingering change in temperament in your horse, consider whether physical pain might be the source of their attitude shift. Anything from an abscess in the hoof to a saddle pinching their back the wrong way can cause a horse to become grumpy, moody, or short-tempered. It's always a good idea to have your vet come out to evaluate your equine friend when things don't seem as they should be.

Sharing your time with a horse isn't just great for your mental health. It can be highly beneficial for your physical health as well. Horseback riding is one of the few activities in which your body is constantly exercising every muscle at once. Much like yoga, you'll need to learn to relax, stretch, flex, and move various parts of your body simultaneously While many non-equestrians will argue that riding is just a matter of sitting on a horse's back while they do all the work, the aching abductors, abdominals, and oblique muscles of any rider who has recently worked on sitting trot will beg to differ.

Even if you don't ride your horse, caring for a horse is still very physically demanding work. A bale of hay can weigh between 50 and 75 pounds. A bag of feed is typically 50 pounds. Water buckets must be dumped and refilled, and manure must be removed, with fresh bedding replaced daily. Moreover, horses ought to be groomed frequently to maintain a healthy coat, which requires vigorous motion in the arms and shoulders. Picking dirt and debris out of a horse's hooves requires bending over and asking the horse to lift each foot. If your horse demands you walk out and personally escort them from the furthest corner of their pasture, you might be getting a good hike in too.

Of course, there's a flip side to every wonderful trait about horses. That long walk to the back of the pasture tends to be a little less enjoyable when it's super hot, raining, or snowing. Likewise, when cleaning stalls in the frigid cold or high humidity, the pitchfork slipping out of your hands can be unbearable. There are flies, spiders, and all sorts of other bugs that you may have never needed to identify until now. Fans and heaters can be helpful, but there's still a lot of outdoor activity when working with horses.

There will be days when you won't want to drag yourself down to the barn to deal with it all. In fact, there will be days when you would rather be anywhere in the entire world than freezing or roasting in a stinky barn. Your back and arms will be sore. You won't be in the mood. You might have a thousand other things to do. But this large beast is depending on you to take care of him.

And yes, there's no denying that horses are not just time consuming but expensive also. Nearly every horse person has gone into the ownership process with the naive thought, "Maybe he'll be an easy keeper! Then I can just feed him a supplemental complete feed, and he can be on 24 hour turnout. All of that grass will keep him fat and happy."

I have had one horse that was an easy keeper. However, since he was out in the field all the time, we had to constantly keep the field mowed so that he wouldn't overindulge in grass and become ill. The fence line had to be checked daily, and any repairs had to be immediate. His water trough still had to be dumped, cleaned, and refilled. His shelter had to be mucked out daily because manure is an ideal breeding ground for flies and other pests.

He had specific health needs as an outdoor horse as well. I had to ensure he was dewormed regularly to prevent parasite build up. Running free and happy in the field caused him to wear down his shoes quickly (or leave them behind in a particularly sticky patch of mud), which meant a pricey farrier bill every six weeks. He was also what we called a "scratch and ding wizard" because he was always coming in from the field with some weird minor flesh wound that would require immediate care.

Therefore, this is your official warning to abandon the hope that your horse will be inexpensive. Feed, hay, bedding, supplements, maintenance of the field and enclosure, vets, farriers, trainers, and all of the supplies such as buckets, wheelbarrows, and pitchforks add up over time. Don't worry. We'll get into a detailed breakdown of costs and equipment in a later section. For now, just rest assured that the old adage is true: There really and truly is no such thing as a free horse.

Horses are also, sadly, very fragile. Their long limbs are easily injured. It's unlikely and even dangerous to ask them to lie down to recover, which means some physical injuries have no hope of healing. They have very sensitive stomachs and are unable to vomit which means a minor tummy ache can turn into life-threatening colic in the blink of an eye. With proper care, horses can live well into their 30s, but one simple accident can end not only their career, but their life.

It's impossible to compare the equine lifestyle to that of any other animal. Horses are amazing companions, providing physical activity opportunities and emotional support for their humans. At the same time, they require full dedication to keep them well. This involves a heavy investment of time and money, which can become very stressful over time. And even when you do absolutely everything right, there are still times when we need to accept that horses are oddly delicate for such large, powerful beasts.

My goal is not to frighten you or make horse ownership sound like a long, miserable disaster. Like any other journey we make in life, there are both wonderful and heart-breaking moments. Some horses live a long, beautiful life without incident, and other horses' lives are cut tragically short. Again, you may ask yourself, "Is it worth it?" I have obviously said, "Yes, it's worth it," several times, but only you can tell if you have the fortitude to take on the responsibility of one of these amazing animals.

SECTION 2: WHAT HORSES REQUIRE OF THEIR OWNERS

When speaking to first-time prospective horse owners about whether they'll be able to provide everything their horse will require, the answer I receive is almost always a version of, "Sure! How hard can it be? We have a shed, a fence, and lots of grass! Everything a horse needs!"

With all due respect to everyone's best intentions, these are actually some of the lower-tier things that a horse will enjoy. While it's true that some horses will be generally pleased with the bare minimum of care, that "bare minimum" may extend much further than you're aware if your horse turns out to have hidden medical issues or personal preferences. Additionally, each aspect of horse care has many considerations that rely on a world of variables. Once you have accepted responsibility for a horse, you'll need to provide the care they require, so it's best to be aware of all of the things that entails right off the bat.

Let's break it down piece by piece:

Water

In an average 24-hour period, a horse will consume between 6 and 10 gallons of water. This can increase dramatically in hot weather or after hard work.

So how are you going to supply this water?

When the horse is relaxing in their stall, a 10 gallon water bucket hung from the wall should be sufficient. You can buy these buckets for a relatively reasonable price at a farm supply store. But, like everything else, there are several things you need to keep in mind.

First, your horse will do everything possible to make his water as disgusting as possible. Nearly every horse person has experienced a horse filling his freshly-cleaned water bucket with manure, often right after it's been topped off. Horses will also stuff their hay and dribble grain in their water buckets, which when left overnight, makes a very strange and stinky brew. If your horse is a "recycler" (i.e.- he eats his own manure), you'll likely have to dump the contents and refill the bucket several times a day. Mares in heat may urinate in their water buckets as well.

Then, you have to consider the critter population of your barn. Despite anyone's best attempts, horse owners are apt to find all sorts of specimens floating in water buckets and troughs. I personally have removed squirrels, baby opossum, mice, toads, moths, wasps, spiders, and even a large and still very much alive cockroach. It is always deeply unpleasant to dispose of these contents, plus, you will need to thoroughly sanitize the bucket before you allow your horse to drink out of it again due to the risks of contamination.

Ofcourse, there's the business of the horse itself. Some horses find water buckets an irresistible play thing. They'll bat them around with their heads, kick at them with their hooves, and rub all of their itchy places against them. You may find your buckets in strange places, or split, spilt, and shattered after no time at all.

If your barnyard has been plumbed with running water pipes and electricity, automatic waterers are a very handy invention. With automatic waterers, you'll never have to worry about your horse running out of water… unless the power goes off for a significant amount of time, or your horse manages to fill it with so much debris that the unit shorts.

These units aren't as portable and easy to dump, clean, and refill as traditional buckets, and they still get their fair share of manure and critter accidents. However, your horse will have constant access to fresh water, and they won't have the option of tossing it out of their stall or stomping it into a million pieces.

For horses that spend a significant amount of time outside, troughs are a popular choice. It would be lovely if horse owners could buy a giant trough, fill it to the brim with water, and not worry about it for a few days. But again, things fall in. From manure to wildlife, a trough needs to be checked several times a day to ensure it's clean.

Furthermore, troughs need to be dumped and cleaned frequently. Much like a pond, or even an aquarium, things start to grow in a trough over time. Regardless of how meticulous you are, it's impossible to escape biology, and you'll find algae and slime coating the inside of your trough after a day or two. For this reason, I recommend buying a trough that you are physically capable of tipping and dumping so you can keep it clean at all times.

Some horses don't mind drinking dirty water. Others will absolutely refuse to touch water if there's a single strand of hay floating in it. Though a horse can survive for days and weeks without food, they can start showing signs of distress after just a day without water. Horses depend on water to keep their digestive systems moving to help flush down the massive amounts of forage they need to stay alive (don't worry- we'll get to the food part shortly). Depriving a horse of water can lead to impaction colic, in which their intestines become blocked, as well as musculoskeletal issues, such as sporadic tying up, a condition in which the large muscles of a horse's hindquarters seem to lock and become painful. Therefore, it is extremely important that a horse has a constant supply of fresh water.

And those of you who live in areas that experience freezing winters will enjoy an extra challenge: ice. Ice will form on water buckets and troughs very quickly. Heated buckets and waterproof heaters that can be dropped into buckets or troughs are available, but these require an electrical source. Some barn owners use a permanently mounted rubber thermal sleeve to prevent ice buildup, and then manually break the ice each morning with a hammer or mallet. I personally find that a well-placed kick on the side of the bucket tends to break up the ice nicely, as well as provides a fun cardio kickboxing type workout, but most people prefer hand tools.

Roughage

Entire volumes have been written about how to feed horses, and truthfully, there is a lot to learn and consider on the topic.

Horses require at least 1% of their body weight in quality roughage each day. When it's cold outside, that number jumps to a minimum of 2%. Working horses will also need more roughage. That means a 1000 pound horse will require 10 pounds of grass and/or hay each day. Bear in mind that a typical bale of hay weighs between 50 and 75 pounds; therefore, a horse can easily munch their way through a bale of hay in a day or two. Use this value to calculate a month's or year's worth of hay to get the full picture of how many hay bales you'll need to keep on hand at all times.

Roughage is non-negotiable for horses. They need it to keep their digestive tract moving. That being said, there are many ways to get the recommended quantity.

First, and least expensive, is pasture. Grass and leafy green things are full of the nutrients horses need to thrive. Your pasture provides the natural diet of horses, and they'll be content to chomp on a field all day. Seems easy enough, right?

Unfortunately, there are quite a few things you'll need to consider before you throw your horse outside all day and wish him happy eating. There are many plants that are toxic to horses and can make them extremely ill or be fatal if eaten. You'll need to take the time to identify which of your area's native plants can be harmful and remove them before your horse is turned out.

There's also too much of a good thing when it comes to horses and food. Horses who eat too much lush grass are at risk for colic. Unlike cows and other ruminants, horses only have one stomach. Ruminants have the ability to regurgitate their cud for additional chewing and digestion, but horses can't regurgitate or vomit at all. As a result, an upset stomach can lead to a full-blown colic episode very quickly.

Laminitis is also a risk for horses who indulge in too much food. The lamina is the soft tissue layer that helps connect the bone of the leg to the hoof. Horses who eat more than their bodies can handle will experience sudden swelling of the laminae. Not only is this incredibly painful, but allowing the condition to continue without treatment can permanently damage the structure of the horse's hoof and lower leg.

Additionally, horses who become overweight are more prone to insulin resistance. Essentially, this is like Type 2 diabetes in a horse. Insulin resistance can also lead to laminitis, as well as excessive drinking, urination, and fat deposits along the neck and hindquarters.

In fact, many experts refuse to allow their horses to graze during afternoons when the sugar content in pastures is at its highest. Instead, they'll turn their horses out overnight, or in the early morning, or evening hours, to ensure they're getting the nutrition they need without worrying about potential overdosing on natural sugars.

The next option for providing roughage is hay. But beware: not all hay is created equally. It's important that you choose hay that has been specifically cut and stored for horses, as this hay will be free of any molds, moisture, or dust that can be toxic to horses. Additionally, there are actually different types of hay. Alfalfa and clover are actually legume hay, while timothy, bluegrass, and orchard are all grass hay. Each type of hay has a different nutritional profile based on the various levels of moisture, crude protein, calcium, and mineral content.

Legume hay is higher in protein and calcium, which means it's richer and denser. Like too much access to pasture, this can cause problems. Some owners have identified that legume hay makes their horses "hotter", meaning they have excess energy. Unless your horse has a hard time maintaining body condition or has a heavy workload, a lot of legume hay can have a similar effect to a large candy bar on a small child.

Grass hay, on the other hand, is higher in fiber but contains lower levels of other nutrients. This means horses have to eat more grass-based hay to get the nutrients they need, but that can be an advantage to horses who spend most of their day inside. The fiber encourages motility in their digestive tracts, which helps mitigate colic and maintain ideal health.

Hay grows in cycles referred to as "cuttings". First cutting produces the early spring hay which tends to be coarse. As the growing season continues, the cuttings tend to be more fine and dense. You may find that you need to feed more of the stemmy, stalky first cutting than the silky, nutritious second cutting and beyond. Older horses with fewer teeth may have difficulty with first cutting hay but will happily munch on second or third cutting hay from the same field.

Generally speaking, hay is easy to come by, but occasionally, environmental factors such as drought or flooding will create a hay blight. You may also find that your horse has a difficult time eating hay, perhaps due to problems with their mouth or teeth, or due to being a choke risk. Just like humans, horses can get food stuck in their esophagus. Unlike in humans, we can't simply perform the Heimlich maneuver on a horse to help them out. They've got several feet of esophagus to coax a blockage through, and then there's the problematic mechanics of that solution.

These are just a few of the reasons that owners might choose to explore different types of roughage. Beet pulp and alfalfa cubes are two examples of commercially available roughage for horses. Beet pulp is often used to supplement fiber intake for horses with a variety of medical conditions that would preclude them from eating hay, including breathing issues, lack of teeth, and metabolic conditions. Alfalfa cubes are used in similar situations for horses who need a denser nutritional content in their roughage supplements. Both beet pulp and alfalfa cubes should be soaked thoroughly before being fed to horses to help them chew and swallow the coarse material.

Grain

A quick trip to the feed mill or farm supply shop will show you that there are seemingly endless options when it comes to a pellet feed for your horse. Choosing the right one may seem like a daunting task.

My personal recommendation is to find out what your horse is eating right now and continue that program, unless you or your vet see any reason to make changes. There are many things that are going to be changing in a horse's life when he leaves his current home to live with you. For example, the pasture and hay will be different. Every experiment requires a control, so my suggestion is to not change grain right away unless there is a very strong reason to do so.

The three main considerations of pellet horse feed are protein, fat, and fiber. There is some debate as to whether horses require more protein or fat, and truthfully, it really depends on the horse and their job. A horse who spends his days leisurely strolling through the pasture will need far less protein and fiber since he's already getting it from the grass. A hard keeping Thoroughbred who loses his marbles and insists on coming inside every time the bugs get aggressive will need far more protein and fiber. He'll likely need more fat too, especially if he's doing a lot of work throughout the day.

Horse feed manufacturers have helpfully labeled their formulas with the type of situation their feed is intended to support. For example, you'll see "Senior Feed", "Mare and Foal Feed", and "High Performance Feed". Always read the tags. Different brands have different formulas, and the levels of nutrition in one brand's "Senior" blend, for example, might be very different from another brand.

One very important thing to note is that the percentages and benefits touted by each type of horse feed are based on the serving directions printed on the bag. If you feed your horse less than the serving directions, you may not see the miraculous advantages claimed by each brand.

When in doubt, talk to your vet. Your vet will be able to look at your horse and evaluate their overall body condition. They'll also be able to take blood samples to find possible nutrient deficiencies.

If you decide to make changes to your horse's feed, remember to go slow. This is true for everything your horse eats including pasture, hay, and hay substitutes. That incredibly sensitive digestive tract that keeps popping up is once again an important reason to slowly make changes to your horse's feed routine. The general guideline is to replace ¼ of a ration per day with the new item, but always check with your vet for specific recommendations.

Medical Care

A solid relationship with a good, thorough veterinarian is essential. Horses are masters of appearing with mysterious maladies. From cuts and scrapes, to lameness and beyond, horses manage to get into all sorts of trouble.

It is a fantastic idea to start hunting for a vet before you even purchase a horse. There may be a variety of vets who service your area, but contacting them before your horse comes home allows you to ensure they are taking new patients and learn more about their practice. Do they have digital imaging equipment? Do they offer dental services? Can they provide chiropractic services? Are they more focused on lameness or reproductive services? How many vets are at the practice? What are their emergency policies and procedures? There is nothing as terrifying as having a horse in critical condition and attempting to frantically connect with a vet in your area.

In addition to tending to your horse in times of crisis, your vet will also be able to provide or recommend deworming programs, vaccination schedules, and long-term care regimens based on your horse's wellness needs. Deworming and vaccinations are very important for a horse's health. Horses can pick up all sorts of parasites when grazing in even the most meticulously kept field, and vaccinations protect against highly communicable diseases that can be spread by common insects and directly between horses. Your vet can advise you as to which dewormers and vaccinations are essential in your area.

In fact, some horse owners prefer to have their vet look at their horse before they even make the first payment. In what is called a "Pre-Purchase Exam," or PPE, the vet will evaluate your prospective horse's conformation, hooves, teeth, conduct a full lameness exam, and may even take x-rays to bring to light any issues that might be lurking in the background. The purpose of a PPE is not to expose the dishonesty of the previous owner, as they may not even know about a horse's issues. Instead, a PPE will prepare you for the level of care a horse will need once it comes home. You will then be able to make a decision as to whether this horse and its needs will fit into your lifestyle and abilities or not.

Once a vet has made their recommendations, a lot of daily medical care for horses can be accomplished at home. You may find yourself cold hosing swollen legs, applying salve and fresh bandages to wounds, or soaking and packing Epsom salts into a lingering hoof abscess. This is all part of the territory when you own a horse. You'll learn how to administer paste medications orally or crush up pills in their feed. You may even learn how to give intramuscular and subcutaneous injections to provide your horse with the treatment they need to stay well.

If you are not comfortable with needles, blood, and assorted bodily fluids, that doesn't mean you can't have a horse. In these instances, you'll want to find someone who can provide 24 hour, 7 day a week support for your horse. A boarding facility that is willing to provide medical care is one option for finding assistance.

Farrier Services

There's a common saying in the horse community: "No hoof, no horse." Truer words have never been spoken.

Foot injuries to a horse are not only painful, but if not attended to can be career ending or even life-threatening. While you can lie down on your sofa with your foot propped up until you heal, horses don't have that luxury. They can lie down, but not for long periods of time. Furthermore, the process of getting up from a prone position requires a lot of effort for horses. You can't just ask a horse to stay off its foot for four weeks.

Therefore, good hoof care is absolutely essential. Hooves are made of a fingernail-like material, and they grow just like fingernails do. When they get too long, they need to be trimmed.

Some people argue that wild horses don't need farriers, so why should their domesticated horses? Wild horses often travel up to 20 miles a day on rugged terrain to find enough food and water, which naturally wears down their hooves. Chances are your horse is not wearing down his feet at the same rate as a wild horse.

Just like humans, all horses move a little differently. If you and a friend bought the same pair of sneakers and wore them for a year, the tread patterns would look different from each other. Your farrier can evaluate your horse's movement and trim their hooves to allow them to move more freely. In fact, a lot of lameness issues can be corrected or relieved with appropriate trimming and horse shoes.

A good farrier won't just trim a hoof; they'll take a look at your horse's conformation, body type, work load, and wear patterns on their hooves or shoes to ensure their work fully supports the horse going forward. They'll evaluate angles and shapes and use a variety of tools to take accurate measurements. I once had a farrier who was able to diagnose my back pain from the wear patterns on my horse's shoes and was able to rebalance both my horse and myself with corrective shoeing. In order to keep your horses healthy, happy, and moving well, a good farrier is non-negotiable.

Attention

For those who find themselves more or less obsessed with horses, this one may seem strange. Who *wouldn't* give their horse endless attention? My experiences have shown me that there are a lot of people who believe horses are field decorations, lawn ornaments, or very pretty lawnmowers. It's not that they dislike their horses, they just don't feel that they require much attention.

When I say "attention", I don't necessarily mean you need to snuggle with your horse all the time. Horses are very social animals. As herd animals, they require some form of interaction. It's not uncommon to find a bonded pair of horses, even in the wild. They create intricate social structures within their herds, and they require some form of interaction in order to be happy. In the absence of an equine companion, horses can bond with other animals such as goats or dogs.

Your experience with your horse will be much more enjoyable if you take the time to form a bond with your horse. There are seemingly infinite "horsemanship gurus" out there who provide tips and tricks for creating the ideal relationship with your horse, but it all boils down to one common action: paying attention to your horse.

The more time you spend with your horse, the more you'll learn about them. Domestic horses tend to be creatures of habit and will develop their own routines. The more you observe and understand their routines, the more likely you will be able to identify when anything is off with your companion. Changes in eating, drinking, manure production, or energy levels can be signs of a medical issue, so catching these strange variances early could save your horse's life.

Take the time to groom them daily. Grooming helps keep the horse's skin and coat healthy and gives you the opportunity to check them over for bumps and cuts or any other unusual skin disturbances. Horses are prone to all sorts of skin issues, such as rain rot, ringworm, and scratches, a type of dermatitis affecting the skin around the lower leg and hoof. These bacterial and fungal infections can cause your horse significant discomfort and can require extensive treatment. The good news is that regular grooming can help you identify these issues at the onset before they become too difficult to manage with over the counter solutions.

Regularly spending time with your horse will also improve your ability to handle them. The easiest way to gain your horse's trust is by spending time with them. Once your horse appreciates who you are and that you have their best interest in mind, it will be much easier to lead them around, hold them for the vet and farrier, and train them to do whatever you wish to accomplish together.

Author's Anecdote: Absolutely Look a Gift Horse in the Mouth… and Everywhere Else

When I was given my Thoroughbred gelding, Red, I knew I had a lot of work to do, but it wasn't until I brought him home that I discovered how much needed to be done. He had been living in a field for four months. He'd had access to grass and water, but that was about it.

Not only did he need to gain about 400-500 pounds to be healthy, but he

was essentially hairless due to the massive coating of rain rot scabs across his back, hindquarters, and barrel. His legs were oozing from scratches sores that had become infected. His teeth and hooves were overgrown, which meant he had trouble eating the food we provided him, and he walked with careful, mincing steps.

I was very careful about introducing grain to him to avoid upsetting his tummy. He got a full round of vaccinations and dewormers. The vet ran blood tests to see what issues he might have and took care of his teeth with a process known as "floating" in which teeth are filed down to create adequate chewing area and take care of any sharp bits that are poking the mouth or tongue. I spent months using medication and special shampoos on his coat to help kill the fungus and regrow healthy skin and hair. He was treated for ulcers, and I gave him supplements designed to help him recover.

All told, bringing Red back to full health required thousands of dollars, several vet visits, and months of careful farrier work. The first few months, I would work a full day at my regular job then drive an hour to the barn where Red was boarded, do my barn chores and spend several hours working with him to clean his skin and build a good relationship with him. It was not easy, and there were several times when I broke down in tears on my long drive home because I wasn't sure how things were going to turn out.

The people who had him before me were not mean people. They had three small ponies who were fat and sassy just as they stood. They simply weren't aware that different horses have different needs. When I pointed out some of the issues Red was experiencing, they were absolutely appalled and ashamed of themselves. They simply didn't know.

Something as simple as spending fifteen minutes a day with your horse can make you more aware of how they're feeling. As you spend time with your horse, you'll notice when they're gaining or losing weight so you can adjust their diet accordingly. When you groom them, you'll feel any changes in the texture or thickness of their coat. Picking their hooves will allow you to assess any cracks, bruises, or abscesses that may need attention.

Today, Red is a thriving middle aged horse. He still requires a lot of work to keep him in good shape. Due to his previous starvation, it's incredibly hard to keep weight on him. But he's an amazing companion-- a sweet, level-headed horse who enjoys cuddles and treats equally. He's spent some time doing equine therapy work with disadvantaged children, and he's even done *some modeling!*

In short, just a little care can go a long way in keeping your horse healthy and happy. That's not to say you have to eat and sleep in your horse's stall or pasture, but you will need to attend to your horse more frequently than you might expect.

If any of these caretaking practices are not ideal for your lifestyle, there are options. The first, of course, is to pass on adding a horse to your list of commitments, but there are situations in which that is impossible. Full board, partial leases, and hiring a caretaker are all ways your horse can get additional attention while you balance the other details of your life. Just remember-- you have a choice in adding a horse to your life, but the horse does not.

Now that you know what a horse needs to stay alive and well, we'll take a look at how to select and create the perfect environment for your horse. Your horse's home is the common factor between all of these caretaking needs and responsibilities, so it's important that your horse's home helps you provide them with all of the things needed to keep them safe and sound for a long time to come.

SECTION 3: CHOOSING THE RIGHT HOME FOR YOUR HORSE

So far, we've mentioned what your horse needs, but we haven't specified where you're going to put everything.

Depending on where you live, this decision may be made for you. If you live in a large metropolitan area, for example, there's no way you can simply make room for a horse in your backyard-- if you even have a backyard. And in suburban areas, zoning regulations and Homeowner Association (HOA) guidelines are likely going to squelch any notion you had of building a stall for your horse in your garage.

However, for those who live outside city limits, the options open up. There are still a few factors that may prevent you from having a horse at home, such as limited land or the expense associated with creating the perfect living arrangements for your horse.

In this section, we'll take a look at exactly what a horse needs when it comes to their living situation. From stalls to fences and everything in between, there are certain things your horse will need in order to be completely comfortable.

As I have mentioned several times throughout this book, always bear in mind that different horses will have different needs. It may seem as though I'm being super repetitive on this point, but even as a seasoned equestrian, it's sometimes hard for me to remember that not all horses are willing to spend half a day outside roaming freely, or that some horses become very anxious if they're kept inside for too long. There comes a point when we've all thrown our hands in the air in exasperation, ditched all of our best intentions, and made do with whatever preferences the horse has.

Therefore, it's important to create a master plan for your horse's habitat with the idea in the back of your mind that you may need to come up with options. We'll look at two scenarios: keeping your horse at home versus boarding him. There are plenty of things to think about in each case, but don't worry- we'll look at the pros and cons of each, as well as create a list of questions to ask yourself and whomever you choose to board with.

Chapter 1: The Ideal Horse Habitat

You've probably heard your horsey friends or trainer joke that the best way to keep a horse would be in a bubble. This is because horses seem to find every possible way to injure themselves when kept in a stall. From finding sharp edges that are unseen to the human eye to getting cast, which is when a horse lies down and can't get up due to how they're wedged against a wall. Horses are very creative at damaging themselves.

Of course, they can find interesting ways to injure themselves in the field as well. Pulled tendons, bruised hooves, and weird scrapes and lacerations are just some of the "fun" things you can find on your horse when you bring them in from the field.

Therefore, the first thing you should ask yourself about any space in which you plan to keep your horse is, "Is it safe?" You don't need a shiny, fancy barn full of giant box stalls, as long as the environment in which you keep your horse is safe. That means fences, stalls, shelters, and even the land itself need to be in good repair. You'll need to check for holes, broken boards and posts, sharp edges, nails or screws that might be poking out, downed branches, leaks, cracks, and so forth. Even a daily microscopic inspection might not prevent some of the mischief horses can get into, but filling in holes in the pasture and testing the fence line is one place to start to mitigate an expensive tragedy.

So how much room do you need for a horse? The general rule is an acre of land per horse, but that only takes into consideration the amount of space a horse needs for grazing. Two acres for the first horse and one acre for every subsequent horse is even better, as this allows the horses room to roam as a herd and cuts back on the risk of overgrazing.

You may look at your field and think, "There's no way a horse could graze that bald," but you might be surprised at what a diligent horse can do to a pasture. Running and rolling will churn up dirt, and when it's wet that means turning a lush pasture into a useless mudpit. If it's very rainy or very dry, your overgrown field can quickly turn into a dirt lot under the hooves and teeth of a horse.

Additionally, there are plants that horses simply will not eat. You'll need to mow or bush hog those from time to time to get them under control. It can be very easy to "lose" a small pony in a thicket of tall weeds. Don't worry-- they'll reappear in time for their next meal, but you'll want to check them over for ticks or other problematic bugs that lurk in the overgrown areas.

From the pasture, we move on to the shelter aspect. Even horses who are content to live outside all day and night will need some form of shelter to protect themselves from the heat, sun, wind, rain, and snow. Depending on your location, you may not experience all of these weather conditions, but horses will enjoy a respite from standing in the open air all day. Whether to get away from insects, or to feel safe while enjoying a nice nap, your horse will be grateful for shelter.

Shelter doesn't always have to mean a stall. Some horses are quite content with a simple three-walled run-in with a roof that protects them from the elements. Others enjoy the security of a stall. The ideal situation is both: a pasture where they can stretch their legs, snack on grass, and socialize, complimented by a large, airy stall in which they can snooze and feel safe.

The size of the stall is also important. An average sized horse of around 1,000 pounds will need a stall that is at least 12 feet by 12 feet. This gives them plenty of room to turn around, lie down, stand back up, and move enough to keep them comfortable. Small horses can get by with smaller stalls, especially if they have plenty of exercise throughout the day.

The main challenge of keeping horses in stalls is boredom. Horses are designed to roam, forage for roughage, and socialize. Unfortunately, it's not always practical to recreate a wild horse's kingdom in our own backyards, regardless of how much land you may have. Most domesticated horses enjoy a balance of turnout in a pasture and time in the stall. This helps landowners rotate pastures between multiple horses or other animals. Plus, it's admittedly very convenient to have your horse in a stall when the vet or farrier is visiting. If you plan on riding or exercising your horse, it's also nice to have a stall or other enclosed space where you can groom them, get them tacked up, and prepare for the work ahead of you.

Again, a stall doesn't have to be a fancy highly-varnished affair. I've seen stalls made out of cattle panels, some constructed from reconfigurable fiberglass and steel bar panels, and homemade stalls from strong posts and 2x6 panelling.

No matter what type of construction you use, airflow in your barn and stalls is extremely important. Horse urine is high in ammonia, and manure doesn't exactly smell wonderful. When it's hot or cold, the air circulation in your horse's enclosure is not only going to keep the stink down, but help you manage the temperature as well. Therefore, if you decide to build a barn or multi-horse enclosure, consider windows or Dutch doors as a way to encourage greater airflow. If you have multiple stalls, consider extending the walls between them high enough to dissuade horses from visiting their neighbors, rather than building them all the way to the ceiling. Many stalls are constructed with bars or mesh across the front to not only allow horses to see out and humans to see in, but to increase air circulation throughout the entire space.

As mentioned, the urine and manure smells will become overwhelming very quickly, so have a plan in place for regular removal and disposal of your horse's waste. Some locations have specific requirements as to where manure can be disposed of in relation to human dwellings, roadways, or water sources, so be aware of those regulations before you start dumping. You may also want to encourage your local gardening friends to tap into your endless source of high-quality organic fertilizer!

Then comes the matter of fencing. The only type of fencing most horse experts would strictly advise against is barbed wire. There are many types of fencing available today, including electrified webbing, high tensile wire, wooden post-and-board, vinyl strips or planks, and more. Some horse owners set up temporary grazing areas with electrified braided rope and QuikFence spikes, even at home, because they're easily moved to prevent overgrazing.

Most horses will respect the visual cue of a fence line, though some require at least one electrified line to remind them to stay within the lines. Also, an electric fence doesn't have to be turned up to extreme levels to coax most horses into obedience. Some barns have solar-powered, portable electric units that are used only when certain horses are turned out or to keep predators out of the field at night. All of this is to say that your fencing doesn't have to be extremely elaborate, as long as it's functional and safe.

The main thing to consider regarding fence safety is how the fencing material will respond if a 1,000 pound beast moving at 25 miles per hour (or faster) crashes into it. There's no way to avoid damage to the fence or your horse, but the type of fencing you have can help prevent tragedy. This is why barbed wire is highly advised against since a horse's body slamming into this type of fencing can result in the horse becoming tangled, leading to multiple lacerations as a possible consequence.

Horses also like to put their heads and hooves through fences. Materials like vinyl and webbing tend to be more forgiving to horses who have this type of tendency. Horses have been known to dangle from a horse shoe or hog-tie themselves in high tensile wire fences. While this is certainly scary for everyone involved and not to be taken lightly, the benefit of this fencing type is that it can be easily cut with heavy duty wire cutters to release the horse and be repaired once the horse is safe and sound. I personally have only had to do this twice in the past 30 years, though my mentor speaks fondly of a horse she had who would get the fence tangled in his shoes at least once a month but had the good sense to stand patiently until someone could pull on the wire to free him.

Therefore, make sure your fencing is safe and that your horse respects it, and choose something that is easily repaired because you may need to repair it more frequently than you might anticipate.

The last element of your horse's ideal habitat is a water source . We've already discussed the importance of your horse having access to water, but let's step back and consider how you're going to get the water to him. Nearly every barn I've worked at, even the small backyard facilities with just two stalls, have a water source inside the barn. This means getting the area plumbed with a spigot or well pump, so you can easily refill buckets or troughs without running back and forth from the house for gallon after gallon of water.

Some smaller facilities have run a very long hose from the house to the barnyard which is also acceptable. The only issue with this plan is making sure the hose doesn't freeze when the temperature drops. If you go with this plan, you might choose to bring the hose inside when it's not in use, or meticulously drain the hose after each use. Heated hoses are another option, though they tend to be a bit pricey.

Natural water sources, such as ponds or creeks, aren't very popular in my area, but I am acquainted with many horse owners in other states who enjoy such amenities. If you are lucky enough to have a reliable natural water source, just be sure to test the water frequently to make sure it's drinkable and inspect the source often. Something as simple and unavoidable as a deer carcass upstream can pollute your horses' water and make them very sick, which means you'll need to be aware and come up with an alternate solution right away.

So there you have it. The basic, ideal horse habitat includes at least an acre to graze and play on, shelter, fencing, and a source of water. It sounds so simple when boiled down to just those elements, yet anyone who has had a horse run through a fence line or get cast in his stall will tell you that these are more than enough features to keep up with at once.

The good news is that you don't necessarily have to do this alone. In some areas, boarding a horse at a professionally maintained facility is a great compromise for those who don't have the time, energy, carpentry know-how, or money to keep their horses at home. Of course, you'll still want to look for these main factors and gauge how appropriate each is for your horse. Let's continue our inspection of horse habitats by looking at the pros and cons of boarding versus keeping your horse at home.

Chapter 2: Should I Keep My Horse at Home or Board It?

Over the past several chapters, we've looked at what a horse needs to be content and in good condition. Now it's time to take a look at the human component of the equine relationship. Armed with these details regarding horse care, how do you feel? Are you as confident and eager as ever to add a horse to your family? Or are you starting to feel a bit of doubt and worry creeping in? Maybe you feel completely intimidated by what you've read so far.

All of these are perfectly natural, and you may experience each emotion in varying waves. After 30 years with horses, I still feel anxious and overwhelmed from time to time, especially when things aren't going according to routine.

The good news is that you don't have to take this on alone. In fact, as mentioned earlier, you may not have the option to do so. Boarding your horse at a facility other than your home can be an amazing opportunity, even if you do have the ability to keep a horse in your own backyard.

Having worked at dozens of facilities, including boarding barns with 100 stalls or more, and small backyard barns housing just a horse or two, I can confirm that there are advantages and disadvantages to both options. Let's take a look at some of the main things to consider when choosing the perfect home for your horse. And for those of you who have no choice but to board, this section will give you some insight into what to look for in a prospective boarding facility.

Advantages of Keeping Your Horse at Home

If you are the type of person who enjoys having control over every aspect of your life, keeping your horse at home may be ideal. When you keep your horse at home, you have around-the-clock access to your horse. If you want to ride at midnight, you can. It's your horse, your property, and your time. You can clean your stalls any time of day and turn your horses out whenever you want. You can set whatever schedule works for you and your horses.

In most cases, you will be the only person to take care of your horse unless you specifically authorize someone else to help you out such as a family member or trusted friend. This means you'll have complete control over the care your horse receives. You can choose how much bedding you put in your horse's stall. You can select what type of hay you purchase, what time of day they get fed, and when they get supplements. You get to put them on the deworming and vaccination schedule of your choice.

Also, you can choose your own farrier, vet, and schedule them whenever your schedules allow. You can select the trainer you want to work with and decide whether you're going to take your horse to their facility for lessons, or whether you want them to come to you. Some trainers will travel, though they may charge an additional fee. The important thing to keep in mind is that you have complete freedom to choose the care team to support you and your horse.

For many equestrians, another advantage to keeping your horse at home is the peace and quiet of solitude. You don't have to share the barn with anyone else. No one will be hanging around, watching you ride, borrowing your equipment, or using the hose when you need to use the hose. If something gets lost, you know exactly who to blame. If you don't feel like talking to anyone, no worries because there's no one around to talk to anyway.

Disadvantages of Keeping Your Horse at Home

If all of that sounds pretty good to you, then you might just be a true dyed-in-the-wool horse person. But hold on, there are a few flip sides to all of those major advantages.

First of all, having complete solo care of your horse means that everything is your responsibility. For example, you'll need to find a hay supplier. You'll need to find a way to get the hay from their field to your barn. You'll need to stack the hay. You'll need to pull bales of hay when it's time to feed them and check them for mold and dust.

You'll need to make all of the decisions in your barn. What type of bedding will you use? Where will you keep it? Where are you going to keep your equipment? How are you going to store your feed? What will your feeding schedule look like? How many hours will you turn your horse out? At what time of day? Where are you going to ride or work with your horse?

The responsibility extends past the mere duties and decisions, and into the expenses. How are you going to pay for everything?

Budgeting for things like a $100 farrier bill each month, a $20 bag of feed each week, and a $6 bale of hay every day is pretty straightforward, but how are you going to budget for unexpected situations? Even the most deliberate budgeting can be thrown for a loop with a $3000 vet bill or $1000 in fence repairs when a storm blows a tree down in your pastures.

You will be responsible for all maintenance too. If you're comfortable with basic tools such as hammers, nails, screws and screwdrivers, hand saws, and wire cutters, you're prepared to handle most of the basics. There's an old saying that "horse people can solve just about any problem with duct tape and baling twine", and to a point, that's very true. Both are strong products that tend to be abundant in a barn setting. When combined with a little creativity and tenacity, they can create a temporary fix for many situations. Check out the Resources section for links giving some insight on this topic, if you're curious!

But real repairs require real supplies,skill, andmoney. You'll need to learn how to repair fence posts and fence lines, stalls, stall doors, gates, gate latches, hoses, water pumps, and more. You'll need to understand how to "horse proof" your property from bush hogging the pastures when they start to grow too high to finding sharp edges in your barn and wrapping duct tape around them. Even things that you think would already be horse-proof can be dangerous. For example, the handle loops on their water buckets can easily jab an eye or scratch their face, so many barn owners wrap duct tape around these loops to prevent injury. As the steward for your horse, it is your responsibility to find these problems, correct them, and deal with the consequences all at once.

You'll also need to find reliable resources for the supplies you need for your horse. That means a regular source of feed, hay, bedding, and footing, if you choose to set up an arena on your property for riding. Bear in mind that feed stores or farm supply shops will run out of your particular brand from time to time. There is a time in each horse owner's life when they stand in silent disbelief at the feed store, dumbstruck by the sight of empty racks where what you need should be. How can they possibly run out of *all* the bedding, feed, or supplement you need? You'll feel yourself break into a cold sweat as you try to consider work arounds, or other nearby supply resources. Are you the type to think fast in situations like this, or will you succumb to anxiety?

Many people avoid this anxiety by buying their supplies in bulk. They buy footing and bedding by the dump truck load and multiple bags of feed at a time. They'll purchase hundreds of bales of hay at once. This is a fantastic idea, as it gives you time to plan ahead for the next time you'll need to stock up. At the same time, it's important to note that all of these things need to be stored in a dry place out of direct sunlight. Do you have room to stack 100 bales of hay? Do you have a large enough airtight, waterproof container to store multiple bags of feed? Buying supplies for your horse in large quantities makes a lot of sense and relieves stress, but you'll need a sufficient amount of room and a plan to keep everything stored appropriately.

Another thing you'll need to plan for is manure management. A 1,000 pound horse will produce over 50 pounds of manure each day. Where are you going to put this waste once it's removed from the stall or the pasture? Occasionally, you can pawn it off on others. Frequently, barns have standing agreements with local farmers that they may help themselves to the manure pile whenever they like. Some horse owners will post "Free Manure" ads on community selling walls and bulletin boards when the pile starts to get out of control. Another option is to buy a spreader attachment for your tractor so you can churn it and cure it in a pasture that is currently out of rotation. That means that your manure would be spread in the field your horses aren't currently using.

In addition to all of these logistics, you'll need to consider your lifestyle. Does your schedule allow you to be at home every day at roughly the same time to keep your horse on a familiar routine? Do you have someone who can help you out if you become ill or injured? Do you enjoy traveling and going on vacations? If having your time available as you wish is important to you, it may not be a good idea to keep a horse at home. However, if your partner or the individuals who share your home are pretty reliable, you can achieve some flexibility. Some families have wonderful bonding experiences when taking care of the horses together. On the other hand, if you already feel stressed from running kids to school and practice, getting to work, getting meals on the table, attending appointments, and more, you might find that adding a horse to the mix only makes things feel more hectic.

Lastly, you'll need to change your insurance policy to account for your horse. What this entails varies greatly from location to location, so if you plan to add a horse to the property on which you reside, be sure to speak to your home insurance agent about next steps. You'll need insurance not just for the property and structures, but for your belongings. Your locality may also require liability insurance for scenarios such as your horse getting loose. You may also need to be insured against any accidents that happen on your property as a result of a guest interacting with your horse, such as a friend getting bitten when feeding your horse a treat. Some states require legal notification signs to be hung in a very visible place, while others require "Errors and Omissions" coverage. Find out what you need to know about insurance before you bring your equine friend home.

Advantages of Boarding Your Horse

As you can gather, having a horse at home will demand a lot from you starting with your time, energy, and money. For this reason, many horse owners -- even those who do have the land and the means to keep a horse at home -- prefer to board their horses at a facility.

The premise for boarding is simple. Find a facility that has available room, and pay a certain amount each month for what is essentially your horse's room and board. There are different types of board, however, so be sure to investigate thoroughly before signing a contract.

- "Full board" refers to a boarding arrangement in which the daily basic needs are taken care of: your horse will be fed the same hay and grain that every other horse in the barn eats at the same time each day by people employed by the barn. Your horse's stall will be cleaned regularly by a barn employee and bedding will be included in your boarding costs as well.

- "Partial board" means that some things are taken care of, but you'll still be responsible for some of your horse's care. This varies from facility to facility. At one of the barns where I've kept my horses, for example, the partial board included twice daily feeding, hay, and bedding, but each horse's owner had to clean their horse's stalls and provide their own grain. If a barn advertises partial board, be sure to ask them what is and is not included.

- "Self-care board" essentially means you're paying for the privilege of keeping your horse at that facility. You'll be responsible for feeding your horse, making sure they have water, sourcing your own hay, and cleaning their stall. You may also be asked to provide your own bedding. In some cases, owners at self-care facilities are asked to turn their horses out and bring them in themselves as well. When you see a barn advertising self-care boarding, assume that you will be responsible for everything involved in the daily care of your horse.

- "Pasture board" means that your horse will live outside 24/7 usually with a herd of other horses. Pasture board can be ideal for some horses, but you'll want to discuss the specifics with the barn owner. Do the horses come in for grain? Are they outside in all types of weather? What if they need to be on stall rest due to a medical situation-- will there be room for them to come inside? How are farrier and vet appointments handled-- will someone at the facility bring your horse in for you? Is there a holding stall or area where you can tie your horse while waiting for your appointment? There are many strategic points that need to be considered with pasture board, but many horses enjoy the ability to roam as they please in their downtime.

As you can see, there are several different types of boarding. Some larger facilities may have all four types of contracts available. Full board is generally the most expensive option, while self-care and pasture board are at the least expensive end of the price range.

But all of these boarding options have a few things in common. Namely, you're not responsible for the facility. You may be responsible for the cost of repairs if your horse kicks through a wall, chews a fence board, or pulls the cross ties out of the wall, to name a few possible scenarios, but the daily ins and outs of keeping the property running properly are not your responsibility. You are not required to make sure the arena has enough footing. You will not need to fix the water pump. You don't even need to care about what happens to the manure after it leaves your horse's stall. When you board your horse, you pay for the privilege of showing up, fussing with your horse as required, and going home.

Additionally, if you choose full or partial board, you pay for the convenience of having feed, bedding, and care of your horse arranged by someone else. This is particularly helpful for those who have very busy or irregular schedules. When you board your horse under one of these arrangements, you don't have to worry about showing up at the barn at 6am on the dot to give your horse his food. You don't have to experience gut-crushing guilt at having to skip a day of mucking his stall. Boarding removes all of the stress of coordinating suppliers, brainstorming creative solutions, and finding the right amount of time to get everything accomplished.

Boarding at some facilities can take a lot of stress out of the horse ownership experience including the vet and farrier care aspect. Many larger facilities have a standing contract with a certain vet practice and local farrier, which means you simply need to contact the barn owner or fill out a sign up sheet when your horse needs its regularly scheduled care. Additionally, in the event of an emergency, you have someone you can contact right away, instead of shopping around for professionals with emergency after-hours services.

You'll also have access to more resources than you might at home. While building and maintaining your own riding area can be expensive and time-consuming, boarding your horse at a barn that already has this considered removes all of that stress. Some barns offer a variety of amenities that horse owners can take advantage of, including indoor and outdoor riding arenas, jumps, barrels, round pens, and trails.

You'll also likely find some very cool bonuses at bigger boarding facilities such as heated tack rooms, wash racks with hot and cold water, view rooms, indoor bathrooms for riders, access to a trailer, onsite horse shows, and more. Some barns are incredibly luxurious with full kitchens, lounge rooms with fireplaces and sofas, and therapeutic massage specialists to attend to your horse each day. Others can only promise you a safe stall and reasonable pasture access. We'll take a look at how to make the right choice for your budget and horse in the next chapter.

Lastly, if you're the type of person who enjoys spontaneously joining coworkers for happy hour, heading out for a romantic weekend getaway, or planning a month-long work vacation to explore South America, boarding your horse offers much more flexibility. In full and partial care situations, you'll just need to let your barn owner know if you're going on an extended holiday. Even in self-care and pasture board situations, you may have some wiggle room in which the barn owner will help out with daily chores for a temporary period at an additional charge.

Disadvantages of Boarding Your Horse

There are, of course, a few downsides to boarding. The first- and most undeniable- concern for many owners is the cost. Depending on where you live, the size of the facility, and the services included, your board costs may run several hundreds or even thousands of dollars each month for each horse. This is the price of convenience.

Most of the time, the cost makes perfect sense. Add up everything you buy for your horse over the course of a month, and you might be shocked at the monthly total. Paying for what you need as you need it may make more sense for your budget than dropping a cool $1,000 at the start of every month. Remember, too, that you're paying for the maintenance of the facility and any fun extras that are included with your board such as bedding or a regular feeding schedule.

Many barn owners live onsite, meaning their home is somewhere on the same property as the barn. This can be great if you want the peace of mind that comes with knowing that if there's an emergency, someone is on hand. Conversely, many barn owners ask that their boarders respect set barn hours. This means you can't run out for a quick midnight ride on your horse without permission. This makes sense, of course, because no one likes to be awoken in the middle of the night by surprise guests, even if they do have a legitimate purpose for being on your property in the middle of the night.

When you board your horse, you must relinquish at least some of the care of your horses. Nearly every barn owner will allow you to feed whatever grain your horse requires to be well, for example, but they might charge an extra storage fee for adding an extra bin to the feed room. You may have to accept that your horse will be turned out when the staff has time to turn him out, rather than going out to the pasture at seven on the dot. You won't have a choice about when buckets are cleaned, what type of fencing is used, or when your horse gets each meal.

This can become very stressful for some horse owners, especially those who are used to taking care of their horses in a very specific way and on a very specific schedule. You will need to make sure both you and your horse are okay with other people handling them, feeding them, and cleaning their stall. If you want to add rubber mats to the floor of your horse's stall, or you don't want them to go outside when the weather forecast is unfavorable, you'll have to coordinate with your barn owner instead of just taking care of it yourself.

At the same time, you'll have more people around. This can be both good and bad, depending on your preferences and the individuals involved. There is something very special about the friendships that can be forged between like-minded horse people. Having someone to help you work through various issues with your horse as your "eyes on the ground" can be incredibly helpful, even if you're working with a professional trainer. Meeting up for trail rides or riding together can bring a new level of excitement to each event. Plus, it's great to have someone you can confide in who understands exactly what challenges and concerns you have regarding your horse.

On the flip side, sharing your space and resources with multiple people can be frustrating. You may arrive at the barn without a minute to spare, only to find that someone else is using the arena. There will always be at least one person who will leave their equipment set up, meaning you'll always have to clean up after them. Equestrians often have very strong opinions about horse care, which means there is eternally some type of gossip or drama amongst boarders. You may come to the barn expecting peace and quiet to enjoy your horse, only to find the barn absolutely buzzing with other boarders doing various things, none of which may be conducive to the solace and serenity you were seeking.

This means you may have a certain sense of pressure to fit in. It is important to remember that you are here for your horse and not to make other people happy. As long as your horse is healthy and happy, you should feel good about yourself. Still, that can be difficult when other people in your barn subject you to a constant barrage of suggestions and criticism. Bear in mind that not every barn will have excessive amounts of drama or cliques. You'll get a feel for who the other boarders are and what is expected of you as a boarder when you tour the facility.

Author's Anecdote: What to Do When You're the Horse of a Different Color

Years ago, I kept Red at a large private facility. The owners had once had a large breeding and showing program but had retired. As a result, they had dozens of empty stalls, a huge indoor arena, an outdoor arena with amazing footing, a well-kept series of trails, and gorgeous pastures. I was introduced to them through a mutual friend, and they agreed that three of us could keep our horses on their property under a self-care arrangement.

I lived more than an hour away from the facility, but the three of us took turns taking care of each other's horses, which made it easier for me. Since they lived closer, they took morning care shifts, and I cleaned stalls and fed in the evenings.

We got along very well with the facility owners, and after some time, they agreed to help us out with things like supplying bedding and turning out our horses for us. It was absolutely ideal for Red and I… until it wasn't.

A well-known local trainer began leasing the facility. She asked the three of us if we would like to leave and seemed surprised when we declined. After all, we'd been there first! Still, the facility was enormous, and I naively figured there was room for all of us.

I was very wrong. Some days, I would find the arena filled with up to ten riders at a time, none of whom were very competent at steering their horses. We were asked to sign an agreement that we could not have other trainers at the facility; only the trainer who was leasing the facility was permitted to give lessons. Even though she and I did not ride or compete in the same discipline, she was adamant that my dressage trainer could not teach on the premises.

Eventually, I was "banished" to the former stud barn. This barn was actually ideal for me because it was a detached structure on the other side of the property. I had a private stall for Red and my own tack room for all of my stuff. He had a giant stall, private paddock, and a giant pasture, which he shared with the yearlings during the day. The downside to this arrangement was that the driveway would flood or ice over during inclement weather, which meant there were days I couldn't get to Red's barn in my car. I started riding Red in the pasture or on the trails instead of in the arena because we couldn't access it.

The trainer asked me every month when I was going to leave because she needed my stall for paying students. I assumed that by sticking to myself, not getting in the way, and keeping everything clean and in good condition, I would be fine. Instead, the trainer and her students became increasingly aggressive in reminding me that I didn't fit in. I didn't ride their discipline, my horse wasn't their preferred breed, and I didn't have a show record to speak of. None of these things were important to me, but they were important to them.

Not every boarding experience will be unpleasant. I currently board my horses in an absolute paradise. All of the riders are the same age and experience level as I am. None of our horses are the same breed. Each boarder has been with our trainer for many years. We aren't in it for the ribbons; we're in it because we love our horses and cherish our experiences with them. We bond over the simple things like finding a great deal on winter blankets. We share many similarities such as an appreciation for classical music and historical fiction. We're no less of a team just because we don't go to shows.

The moral of this story is that not every boarding experience is going to be the same. It is absolutely vital to visit every boarding facility that interests you to get a feel of the environment and vibe. Talk to the other boarders. Meet their horses. What types of disciplines are ridden? Can outside trainers teach on the property? Does the facility host onsite competitions, clinics, or camps? What provisions do they offer for boarders who prefer not to participate in those activities? What types of riders are at the facility-- professionals, adult amateurs, juniors, or are the riders mostly casually interested in having fun with their horses?

It is possible to get along with a horse of a different color, but many boarders find that life is a lot more peaceful when they board with like-minded individuals. Red and I learned a lot from our experience at that facility-- specifically, what type of environment we don't enjoy. I recommend boarders caught in similar situations always take the high road, and remember there are always people like you out there. They may not be at the same barn right now, but they are out there. Keep your head high and seek out better options.

Chapter 3: Things to Ask Yourself When Deciding to Build or Board

There have been a lot of concepts thrown around in the past two chapters, and your head may be spinning with "if-then" concepts and trying to juggle many different possibilities at the same time.

Deciding whether you want to build your own facility to keep your horse at home versus paying to board your horse on another person's property truly can be confusing, emotional, and frustrating. Therefore, this chapter is intended to outline the questions you need to ask yourself before you make your final decision.

If you decide to board your horse, there will also be another myriad of questions you may potentially ask. Those questions tend to stray a bit from the intended purpose of this particular list, but as they are no less important. I have added them within the Resources section. For the time being, however, we'll focus on making the first big decision: to keep your horse at home or board them.

Let's start with your budget:

- How much will it cost to build a safe and comfortable home for your horse?
- What insurance considerations and expenses would you incur housing a horse at your home?
- Do you prefer to pay a set amount for all of your expenses each month, or take care of expenses as they occur?
- Do you have adequate savings to cover an unexpected situation like repairing a fence line or stall?

Next, let's look at your time constraints:

- Are you able and willing to be available to your horse around the clock?
- Can you adhere to a strict daily routine of feeding, cleaning up after, and attending to your horse's needs?
- Is traveling or living spontaneously important to you?
- Alternatively, do you have someone reliable who can help you

care for your horse when you are otherwise occupied?

Now, consider your overall enthusiasm about the following tasks. Remember you will be doing these chores in every type of weather applicable to your location:

- Daily stall cleaning-- removing several pounds of manure and replacing soiled bedding
- Lifting, stacking, and separating hay
- Dumping, scrubbing, and refilling water buckets
- Checking every inch of fencing

Can you provide the following resources to help keep your horse comfortable and healthy?

- Water source
- Electricity
- Manure management system
- Pasture rotation strategy

Last, but certainly not least, take a minute to consider your horse's preferences:

- Does your horse require a lot of time outside to maintain their sanity, or do they hate turnout?
- Does your horse enjoy being in a herd environment, or do they prefer to be less social?
- Does your horse have a hard time adjusting to new environments?
- Does your horse require specialized care that would be unavailable either at home or while boarding?

When considering these questions, bear in mind that there are no wrong answers. As long as you keep your horse's health and wellness as the primary consideration in answering these questions, you are doing the right thing.

It might surprise you to learn that some horse owners who have a facility at their home often decide to temporarily board their horses. There are many reasons why they might decide to do this including taking advantage of the seasonal amenities such as a heated barn in the winter or a fantastic trail system in warm weather. They may also want to take advantage of daily training with a professional, or may board only when the horse or human is recovering from an injury or illness, or during construction/maintenance/updates to the home barn.

When you make the decision to keep your horse at home or board him, you're not required to stick with your decision forever. As long as you have access to a trailer or hauling service, you can move your horse as much as your budget and his tolerance for trailer rides and routine disruptions permits.

These are not easy questions to answer. There will obviously be days when you don't feel like getting out of bed before the sun. You'll sweat, freeze, and be frustrated and uncomfortable. However, in order to provide the best possible lifestyle for your horse, you need to be honest with yourself: is this something you are willing to do, or is it best left to the professionals? Your horse will thank you just as much for your honesty as he will for the care that allows him to thrive.

SECTION 4: PREPARING TO CARE FOR A HORSE

So far, we've taken a look at the considerations of having a horse, including what they'll need to be happy and healthy, along with what a perfect home for a horse would include. We've discussed whether it would make more sense for you, your horse, your budget, and your capabilities to keep that horse at home, or board it at another facility. We've also examined some of the major pros and cons of each option.

Compared to the number of variables and potential decisions to be made in the previous sections, this section is "easy." At this point, you've found the ideal horse, you've got a solid grasp on the various aspects of horse care, and you know where your horse is going to live. Now you just need to get that space ready for your horse's arrival and prepare for the first few days, weeks, and months following your horse's entrance into your life.

The days leading up to -- and even a few days following -- your horse's arrival may be very stressful. The intent of this section is to help you gain footing on what needs to be done and how to get it accomplished. There are a lot of moving parts as you organize for transport, so it's important to stay focused so you can complete each step along the way.

Once it's all over and your horse is relaxing contentedly, you'll have a much clearer picture of the amazing relationship you're about to forge with this very fascinating creature. But in the meantime, it's going to be a lot of finding, organizing, cleaning, signing, and planning.

Author's Anecdote: Horse Owners Are Very Stable People

I've had the pleasure of having numerous equine companions. Each time, the experience was a little different. When I bought my first horse, his previous owner threw in all of his equipment from the open bag of treats to his custom-fit saddle. I didn't need to pay for anything but the horse himself and the first month of board.

Red was a spontaneous purchase. He was in such terrible condition that I wasn't sure what I would need, so I showed up with a halter and lead rope and headed to the tack shop afterwards. Each horse that I've rescued has been somewhat spontaneous and needs-based, so I generally have little time to prepare. But one horse stands out as being the purchase I was least prepared to make.

I had seen a horse online that struck a note with me. I wasn't sure why, but there was something very special about this horse. I conversed with his current owner via the sales site, and I got a feel for what was going on. She no longer had the resources to continue to care for him, and he needed a new home by the end of the month. To complicate matters, she shared this detail with me just two weeks before the month was ending.

I was out of the state at the time, and I was unable to leave my current location in time to bring this horse home. My trainer was happy to provide a stall for him, but I coordinated his trial ride, purchase, transport, Coggins, and initial health examination all via email or phone. It's commonly said that you should never buy a horse sight-unseen, and I agree wholeheartedly, which is why I relied on a trusted equine professional to evaluate and provide her own review of the horse before I made the purchase.

Thankfully, everything went off like clockwork. Everyone was on time and courteous, and my horse made it home right on schedule. I was very excited to meet him for the first time a few days later. He's currently making a splash in the eventing world and having the time of his life.

I wouldn't recommend this process to anyone who hasn't completed the process several times before. It's important to make sure everyone communicates and that you're thoroughly prepared to be present for as many steps in the process as possible. Someone could have swapped out the horse I bought for another horse. The transporter could have been less honest about the time frame of travel or the costs. Both barn owners needed to be present to sign off on the transport as well. Meanwhile, I was glued to my phone trying to make sure every step went smoothly.

I highly encourage you to get everything ready ahead of time. Buy all of the supplies you need or think you might need. Contact all of the professionals *you'll want on your team. Plan out your routines, and get an idea of what your horse is going to need from the moment he steps off the trailer going forward. Sure, there will be bumps in the road and last minute changes, but having clear expectations will make adjusting to the "horse life" that much easier.*

Chapter 1: Things You'll Need before Your Horse Arrives

Some people love shopping while other people would rather participate in any other activity. Therefore, it is either very good news or very bad news that you will need to go shopping before your horse arrives at your home or at its new boarding facility.

The good news is that there are many places to source the items you'll need. Feed and farm equipment stores, such as Tractor Supply Company or Rural King, will often have all of the required items, along with a few extras that your horse may appreciate. If you have a nearby feed mill or tack shop, these are also great places to find what you and your new buddy will need.

Online shopping is also a wonderful option. Many online equine retailers offer free shipping for orders over a certain amount, which can be helpful when you're shipping several hundred or even thousands of dollars in supplies at once. Most carry an amazing array of products, from a package of eye hooks that can support the weight of a ten gallon water bucket, to a brand new show saddle.

Of course, it's easy to get carried away when it comes to shopping for your horse. Monogrammed saddle pads, coolers, and winter blankets may leap out at you from the web pages as you scroll. Equestrians have a tradition of color-coordinating all of their horses' clothing, from bell boots and polo wraps to the rhinestones in the browband of their bridles, so you may be blown away by the sheer volume of options you have.

For the most part, the least expensive options will be sufficient for a first time horse owner. While the differences in quality between a $20 halter and a $120 halter will be obvious to you, they really aren't that important to the horse. When shopping, look for products that are safe and durable. You can always buy what you need now and save up to splurge on more expensive products you desire later.

There are a few places where you should not compromise, however. Brand new saddles that retail under $200, for example, should be thoroughly examined before you spend your money. Many of these are constructed of poor quality leather that rips easily. Additionally, the interior construction of the saddle may not be very durable. Often, these saddles start leaking padding or the tree which supports the rider's body will crack.

On the flip side, the internet is a great place to find used and consignment tack and equipment. Sites like eBay and Facebook Marketplace are great places to find amazing deals on horse equipment. Nearly every equestrian will tell you of an enviable purchase they made through sites such as these, and the good deals aren't hard to find if you know what you're looking for. Sometimes national retailers such as SmartPak, Dover, Chick's, and State Line Tack will sell their floor samples which can be another way to get great deals on slightly used high quality equipment.

Local tack swaps and sales are another way to find necessities at a fraction of the price. Often, these events will be hosted by a local 4-H group or riding club, so stay tuned to your local events calendar to find a tack swap near you.

So what types of equipment do you need to have on hand prior to your horse's arrival? I recommend having the following items at a bare minimum:

Equipment for Feeding and Watering Your Horse:

One plastic 8 quart bucket for water

One plastic bucket or rubber pan for feed

One three quart feed scoop

A heavy duty hose

Rubber or metal stock tank to serve as a water trough in the pasture

Dish soap and toilet brush for cleaning buckets

Exceptions: Some stalls have built-in feed dishes and/or automatic waterers. In this case, you may wish to have a spare bucket on hand in case the power goes out or for soaking injuries, but it isn't an immediate requirement. Additionally, those who choose to board their horse may not need to provide these items if they're already installed.

Equipment for Handling Your Horse:

One halter

One lead rope

One lunge line

Note: Halters can be made of many materials including nylon, rope, and leather. Some barns require horses to wear "breakaway" halters as a safety measure. These are halters with a leather crown piece that is designed to snap if your horse gets caught on something. Don't worry- you can purchase additional crown pieces so you can keep using the same halter. All leather halters will function in the same way, but full nylon and rope halters will not yield in the event of a struggle.

Equipment for Mucking Stalls:

A wheelbarrow or wheeled hand cart for muck buckets

One plastic manure fork

One rake or metal-tine fork

A heavy duty shovel

Note: The bigger the wheelbarrow the more you can pull out of your

horse's stall at once, but the heavier it will be. Make sure you can safely handle your stall mucking equipment when it's full to avoid making a stinky mess in the barnyard.

Equipment for Grooming:

One rubber curry comb

One rubber grooming mitt

One soft body brush

One stiff body brush

One hoof pick

One hoof brush

One heavy duty comb for mane and tail

Fly spray

Equine shampoo

Conditioner for the mane and tail

Baby oil

Several towels

Note: Shampoo, conditioner, and baby oil may seem unnecessary if you're not planning to show your horse. However, all three of these products will come in very handy for horses that spend a lot of time outside. They easily remove caked on dirt and mud. Baby oil is particularly helpful for removing burrs, thistles, and thorns from manes and tails without damaging the hair.

First Aid Kit:

Multiple rolls of 4-inch self-adhesive bandage tape (such as Vetrap or Vet Flex)

One set of standing wraps

One roll of cotton wool

Multiple rolls of gauze

Petroleum jelly

Thermometer with retrieval clip

Sanitary pads or baby diapers (great for placing medication or pressure on wounds!)

Rubber gloves

Duct tape

A tube of Banamine*

A tube of Bute*

Epsom salts or Epsom paste

Antiseptic wound cream

may require vet approval for purchase; pay attention to storage requirements

Note: There are several other topical wound treatments that you may need to add such as Fura-zone, Betadine, Swat, or Wonder Dust. These are very helpful treatments to have on hand for various stages of wound treatment that may not be necessary in an emergency situation. Invest in these products as you can-- they typically have a long shelf life if stored correctly.

Storage Solutions:

One heavy duty sealable, moisture-proof container per type of grain/supplement

One sealable, moisture-proof container for the first aid kit

Hooks for hanging up halters/lead ropes/lunge lines that are not in use

Racks or bins for storing clean blankets (one per blanket)

Note: As mentioned earlier, grain cannot be stored in its bag as the

bag is generally not moisture proof. Additionally, wildlife, insects, and the horses themselves will be very interested in having access to all of your feed components. This is why heavy-duty, sealable containers are recommended. Examples include pest-proof garbage cans, lockable plastic trunks, or metal containers that can be latched. Some people repurpose old chest freezers to hold their various animal feeds. You can also find bins and containers specifically designed for livestock feed.

In addition to these very necessary items, there are many items that will be helpful for both you and your horse. I consider these items "optional" because they may or may not be necessary depending on your location, whether you board or not, and your current and future plans for your horse. These include:

- Heavy duty stall fans
- Horse-formulated salt and mineral blocks
- Heated water buckets
- Ladder or step stool
- Fly predators
- Tack, including:
  - Saddle
  - Bridle
  - Bit
  - Reins
  - Saddle pad
  - Girth or cinch

A Word about Blankets

I'd also like to take a moment to speak briefly about blankets and blanketing. The topic is so extensive and passionately discussed that it could be a separate book altogether. However, as a person new to horse care, you'll want to know the basics.

There are many different types of horse blankets, and your horse may require all of them or none at all. Your horse may come with his own full wardrobe, depending on the seller. These are some of the more common blanket types you may find:

- **Cooler:** a thin blanket designed to wick away moisture and prevent a hot and sweaty horse from getting too cold too quickly. These are generally designed to be worn for a short period of time and do not have straps or fasteners, which means you won't want to leave them on an unsupervised horse. Horses are pretty good at taking off blankets on their own and will deposit unwanted blankets on their stall floor. It's much easier and less messy for a human to remove it for them.

- **Stall sheet/Stable blanket**: a thin blanket to provide warmth and moisture wicking to prevent overheating. These generally have adjustable straps at the belly and neck so that horses can wear them for a longer period of time without removing them. They are not waterproof or durable, however, so a horse who is turned out in a stall sheet may find creative ways to destroy it.

- **Rain sheet**: a true rain sheet is simply a waterproof blanket which fastens at the neck and under the belly. These are often tear resistant and appropriate for turnout.

- **Turnout sheet**: these are the most durable of horse blankets. They are waterproof and insulated. They are rated by weight, which corresponds to how much insulation they contain. A lightweight blanket contains 150 to 250 grams of fill, which is appropriate for temperatures below 40 degrees Fahrenheit. A medium to heavyweight blanket contains 250 to 300 grams of insulation, and a heavyweight blanket can range from 300 to 400 grams of filling. Many have leg straps to help them stay in place while your horse runs and plays in the field.

- **Combination sheet**: this is a pair of blankets sold as a set. The most common combination is a medium or heavyweight stable blanket with a rain sheet. These blankets typically have extra fasteners and straps to keep them connected to each other when used as a pair though they can be used separately.

- **Fly sheet/Scrim**: this is a very thin sheet used for protecting sensitive horses from fly bites during seasons where the pests are at their worst.

Blankets are sized by measuring from the center of the chest, over the shoulder and belly, and to the point of the rump under the tail. A horse who measures 72 inches from chest to rump will wear a size 72 blanket, for example.

Blankets can cause chafing if they're too tight or are worn for a long period of time. Sleazys, slinkys, and slickers are all names of Lycra products that can be slipped over a horse's head and under a blanket to alleviate chafing. These types of hoods are also used to keep horses clean and well-groomed before a show. They look a bit silly at first glance, but they can be very helpful in avoiding painful blanket rubs. They are also not always waterproof, so you may want to double check that fact before turning your horse out in the snow, rain, or mud.

In warm weather, you may want to provide your horse with a fly mask as well. Insects love horses, but horses do not return the sentiment. You may be surprised at the number of insects that will buzz around your horse's face. A fly mask is a type of mesh covering that wraps around a horse's face. They are available in almost infinite styles and colors and patterns, including pull-on, Velcro-fastened, over-the-ear, without ears, padded, and so on. If your horse is being bothered by bugs, a fly mask is a great investment.

Some horses have sensitive coats and skin and require a variety of different blankets. Some require none at all. Pay attention to whether your horse appears to be uncomfortable or too cold, with signs such as shivering, pawing, a tucked tail, or even refusing to drink water. Feel their ears and chest. If they feel cold to the touch, this can also indicate that your horse may be chilly.

At the same time, remember that most horses grow a winter coat to help them stay warm. Unless you clip your horse to keep him from overheating in his naturally created winter coat, he should be pretty good at moderating his own body heat in a variety of temperatures. There are, of course, exceptions to this theory, so always put eyes and hands on your horse to make sure he's comfortable.

Keep in mind also that these are just some very basic guidelines for what you'll want to have on hand. Over time, you will most assuredly acquire a number of items that are a little more "want" than "need." Horse owners are often accused of "hoarding" equipment. There may be a little truth to that, but the fact is that multiples of some items are more than warranted. Saddle pads, for example, get sweaty and dirty quickly, and often require air drying. Therefore, having several on hand is not a bad idea. Another example is the manure fork. Despite our best efforts, these do break and bend, and given their purpose in the barn, must be replaced immediately. Having a backup fork is good planning. Multiple manure buckets or wheelbarrows can also be helpful, especially if you have several stalls or a long haul to the manure pile.

Of course, you may choose to add and delete from these suggestions as necessary, depending on your situation. If you are boarding your horse, you may be required to use a certain type of feed storage solution, and you likely won't need to supply your own hose, for example. Always double-check with the barn owner as to what equipment you are expected to bring. This and other questions are addressed in the "Questions to Ask a Prospective Boarding Barn" portion of the Resources section.

Chapter 2: Moving a Horse Into a New Space

Bringing a horse home for the first time can bring about many emotions. It's very exciting, of course, but it can also be cause for great anxiety, especially if this is your very first time adding a horse to your life. There are a few things you can do in preparation of the big day that will help things move along more smoothly.

The first thing to work out is how your horse is going to get from wherever it is now to its new home and whether that home is going to be on your own property or at a boarding facility. After all, it's not like you can just ride a horse down the interstate!

If you do not already own a trailer or have one at your disposal, you will need to arrange a trailer to pick up and deliver your horse. Years ago, I was lucky enough to have a barn owner who had her stock trailer constantly hitched to a capable dually truck. I just needed to text her to tell her when I needed it and where I was taking it. I had to have a copy of my insurance information on file with the office, and I was expected to return it with a full tank of gas. Today, however, I don't have that luxury, which means relying on friends or horse shipping services as necessary.

No matter where you source your trailer, there are a few things you need to keep in mind. First, ask what type of trailer it is. Ramp trailers have a built-in ramp that lowers to allow the horse to easily walk up into the trailer. Step-up trailers are named because there is no ramp, and your horse will literally have to step up into the body of the trailer.

A stock trailer is big and spacious, as it's designed to accommodate a variety of livestock. Some horses actually prefer these trailers since they don't feel overly cramped or confined. Trailers designed specifically for horses often have permanent dividers that help encourage the horse to stay standing. A small window will help keep air moving through the trailer during transit. Always remember to shut the window or put up the screen guard before you start driving. Letting your horse hang his head out the window while zooming down the freeway is incredibly dangerous.

Of course, if you're buying a horse from another state or region, you may not be there in person to load your horse and make the journey home with him. If you are using a shipping service, or hiring someone to bring your horse to you, make sure you ask how often they will stop for hay and water. If the trip is very long, where will they be overnighting? Will your horse have the opportunity to get out of the trailer to stretch his legs?

Travelling via trailer isn't exactly easy for horses since they need to stand and balance in the trailer for the duration of the trip. Your horse may come off the trailer a bit lethargic and possibly even a bit dehydrated, depending on the length of the trip. Conversely, he might be very excited to meet everyone in his new home and bounce off the trailer merrily while loudly announcing his arrival to anyone in earshot. Be prepared for either response, and consider parking the trailer in a spot where you can easily shuttle the horse into his stall or a safe paddock after unloading.

Before your horse comes home, you should request any medical paperwork you need, such as a health certificate or Coggins test result. You also have the right to ask about any prior reports, such as x-rays or reports following a major injury or illness. At the very least, try to get the dates the horse was last dewormed, along with the dewormer they received. Also ask about vaccinations-- when did they receive them, and which ones were they given?

This is important to ensure your horse is starting off his new life with you on a healthy note. Deworming is necessary to flush the horse's system of any intestinal parasites which shed through passing manure. Some parasites are normal since horses often eat in the same area where manure is passed. However, not all dewormers are the same. Some deworming products are relatively gentle, while others must be given at precise dosages for the horse's safety. It's important to know which your horse has received, and how recently, to avoid intestinal upset.

You'll also want to speak with the previous owner about any stall vices your horse may come with. The term "stall vices" sounds a lot worse than it is, but many of these can be very concerning for a first-time horse owner. As noted in the beginning of this book, not all horses are necessarily thrilled about spending the day in a stall, so some of them develop bad habits as an outlet for their energy and emotions.

Cribbing is considered one of the most "unforgivable" stall vices because it is a very hard habit to control, and can cause significant damage to your horse and their habitat. A horse who cribs will latch his teeth onto a solid surface, usually a piece of fencing, a gate, or a ledge in his stall, and suck air through his mouth. When the horse does this, it releases endorphins, so the horse becomes more or less physically addicted to the practice. It not only makes a really annoying "HRUNK" noise, but can lead to the development of ulcers in the horse, and can lead to damage of the surfaces he uses to crib on. Horses don't enjoy the action so much as the flood of endorphins, but many will crib relentlessly until the habit is under control.

The good news is that there are many types of cribbing collars available through equine retailers. These simply buckle around a horse's neck at the jaw and allow the horse to eat and breathe naturally. When the horse attempts to suck air after latching to a solid surface, the collar will not allow them to inflate their windpipe. A grazing muzzle is also a good choice for a cribbing horse. There are some commercially available pastes and bad-tasting goos that can be applied to surfaces to dissuade cribbing as well, but a really enthusiastic cribber will find a way to work around these.

Wood chewing is a similar issue, though harder to control. A horse who chews wood is often more bored than hungry, though supplying loads of hay can often keep them occupied. Stall toys are one way to keep a horse from becoming too bored, along with regular exercise and turnout. A wood chewer may need to wear a grazing muzzle in a boarding barn to keep him from gnawing his entire stall down. Splinters in the mouth, esophagus, stomach, and intestine can be very dangerous, in addition to the inconvenience of eating holes in his habitat, so wood chewing should be controlled and limited as quickly as possible.

Weaving and stall walking are similar habits in that they involve hyper activity within the stall. Horses who weave stand still and sway from side to side. Stall walkers, on the other hand, obsessively trudge in circles in their stalls. Neither of these is particularly dangerous for the horse, but your horse will go through bedding much more quickly than one who spends more time standing still.

The number one way to deal with these stall vices is through exercise and turnout. Each of these is a clear sign that the horse is stressed out in his stall, so spending constructive time outside of the stall will help relieve that stress. That's not always practical, however. This is why it's a good idea to ask the previous owner about any stall vices before your horse arrives. The previous owner can tell you what to expect, how they've dealt with it in the past, and make any recommendations going forward.

Once your horse is in his new home, you'll want to be cautious about introducing him to other horses. Though horses are by nature very social creatures, some of them don't make a great first impression, especially when they're already excited or stressed out from a trailer ride. On the other hand, some horses will go to great trouble to join the herd as quickly as possible by hopping the fence, or unlatching their stall door to meet their new friends.

Horses meeting each other for the first time typically make a lot of strange noises. There may be pawing, kicking, rearing, and striking at each other. Many experts recommend introducing horses through a safe barrier, such as the front of a stall. Meeting through the fence is pretty common also, but it's important to monitor them during the process, as a flailing hoof can easily get stuck in the fence. Bites and kicks are normal, but it's important to assess any damages immediately. Tiny nicks and bruises should heal naturally, but giant bite wounds and lacerations will require immediate vet attention.

There is honestly no way to accurately predict how horses are going to react to new friends and neighbors. Red, for example, has been turned out with other geldings, mares, foals, and stallions with equal success; however, he will chase any grey or light colored horse. As a thoroughbred, he has both the speed and endurance to run the poor pony ragged, so ideally, he's only turned out with darker horses. On the other hand, he loves miniature horses and will protect them from any more aggressive horse who might try to bully them. I can't explain it, but I do my best to accommodate his preferences for everyone's safety.

Over time, you'll learn more about your horse, including his likes, dislikes, and preferences. The first 24 hours are a critical time for building this understanding, as well as developing a relationship. While it's certainly not always practical to camp out in your new buddy's stall for a full day, there are a few things you'll want to pay attention to over the course of the first few hours and days. Here are a few specific things to note as you get to know your equine companion:

- When does he drink the most water? Many horses drink throughout the day, but some horses will guzzle their water right after feeding.

- Does he eat his hay enthusiastically, or pick at it? If he leaves his hay, does he finish it eventually, or throw it out of his stall/urinate on it/stuff it in his water bucket?

- Where does he choose to urinate/leave manure? Some horses prefer to keep their waste in a specific corner of the stall, while others just don't seem to care.

- How often does he produce manure? Is it solid or loose? Some horses will have loose stool after a stressful event like moving, but it should stabilize within a day.

- Does he enjoy rolling in his stall? Horses love to roll in fresh shavings, mud, and dirt, but it can be easy for a horse to get cast in his stall, meaning he wedges himself up against the wall and can't flip over. When this happens, humans need to help them reposition themselves to get up.

- Does he have good stall manners, or does he pin his ears or snap at other horses and people as they walk past his stall?

These are just a few good notes to have in mind going forward with your new horse. You want to get a baseline understanding of your horse, so you can know when they're acting strangely, as unusual behavior can be a sign of health problems. You may also wish to take your horse's temperature, so you know what "normal" looks like in your horse.

With this said, understand that your horse is a living being, and may vary his routine from time to time. However, if your horse normally drinks an entire bucket of water in the evening, but in the morning his water is completely untouched, this could indicate a problem. A horse who normally doesn't roll in his stall who is suddenly lying down and doesn't want to get up could be displaying symptoms of several issues. You need to get an idea of your horse's normal range of behaviors so that you can identify abrupt changes that may be indicative of a serious issue.

Chapter 3: Establishing Your Routine

One way in which you can start to get a feel for what your horse's "normal" is, is by establishing your horse care routine. This will help you track any changes as the days go by as well as provide a steady schedule for your horse. Horses definitely learn to appreciate repetition. Much like any other animal, ourselves included, they can be trained to expect meals and activities at a certain time.

If you choose a full board situation for your horse, you won't necessarily need to create a routine so much as learn the order of operations for that particular facility. It's generally good etiquette to not show up in the middle of feeding time and expect to ride without clearing it with the barn owner, for example. Not only do you risk getting in the way and interrupting whatever process is going on, but your horse might be miffed about having to miss a meal.

For those who do keep their horses at home, establishing your routine is going to require some trial and error at first. You'll want to give yourself a comfortable time cushion before you have to be anywhere, in case the unexpected happens. The "unexpected" could range from a horse coming in from the field with a wound, to a water bucket breaking and requiring immediate replacement. This type of thing will almost always happen when you're rushing because you need to be somewhere, so plan ahead to give yourself some extra time.

Most horses who live in stalls enjoy at least two feedings a day consisting of hay, grain, and water. You'll want to choose the amounts you serve based on your horse's body condition and needs, as discussed earlier, which means you may want to keep hay in front of your horse's face any time he's not turned out in the field. On the other hand, if he's the type to waste his hay, you may want to dole it out just a little bit at a time, so it doesn't end up trampled and covered in manure.

You'll want to check your horse's water source several times a day to make sure that he has enough to drink and that it's clean and fresh, and he hasn't done something to make it gross. Be sure to dump and scrub water buckets regularly.

If your own schedule permits, consider cleaning your horse's stall while he's turned out in the pasture. This way, you can take your time and thoroughly clean up any manure and urine in the stall.

Some horses are impeccable housekeepers. They'll deposit their manure in one corner and urinate in one spot exclusively. These stalls are lovely to clean because you simply take out the bad and put in clean bedding.

Then you have horses who are very active in their stalls and manage to make it look like their stall hasn't been cleaned within an hour of stripping it to the floorboards and refilling it with clean bedding. I have had several horses like this-- at one point, a partial care barn owner took me aside to beg me to clean Red's stall more often. I had just cleaned it two hours prior. He had just managed to urinate in the middle and churn up the bedding into a damp, stinking mess in those two hours.

In my opinion, the best thing about stall cleaning is that, as long as you get everything dirty out and replace it with fresh bedding, there's no "right" or "wrong" way to do it. If you are new to cleaning stalls, I recommend starting with the obvious and sifting down to what's hidden. That means pulling out the piles of manure that are on top of the bedding first, then sifting through the remaining bedding to discover bedding that's soaked with urine or has been churned under a clean layer from the horse walking around, lying down, or dropping hay on top.

One popular question is, "How long does it take to clean a stall?" It really depends on the horse and how well the stall has been maintained. A horse who is a tidy keeper, who is turned out all day or all night, or who's stall is cleaned every day may just have a few piles of droppings and a single patch of urine to remove. This could take just a matter of minutes to remove. On the other hand, a horse who is on medical stall rest, who must stay in all day, may have a stall that defies reason and could require up to an hour to fully sift through.

Another common question is, "How much bedding should I put in my horse's stall?" The main goal of bedding is to absorb the moisture and smell of manure and urine, so you'll want to be sure there's enough bedding that your horse isn't trying to coexist with a giant puddle. Four to six inches of bedding is considered standard for a stall in which a horse spends a lot of time, while two to four inches may be preferred for horses who spend most of their days and nights outdoors.

Additionally, consider how much time he spends in his stall and the barn foundation. If the barn has a hard cement foundation, you might want to increase the bedding to make it more comfortable for your horse to stand on it most of the day. If you have rubber mats in your stalls, that can provide additional cushioning to make standing a little more comfortable. You will most likely need to experiment with bedding levels until you get the right amount down to a science.

As to what type of bedding you should use, the only absolute, firm, non-negotiable bedding to avoid is black walnut wood shavings. Black walnut can create an almost immediate laminitic response in horses. If you work with a local sawmill to use their discarded shavings, make sure they do not process black walnut wood.

Otherwise, there are many different types of products available. You can find very fine, dust-like shavings. These are easier to pick through with a manure fork, but tend to be so good at their job that they'll absorb ambient moisture. Some types of shavings will turn black the minute they get even a little damp. This doesn't impact their ability to do their job at absorbing the dampness and smell of manure and urine, but it does give a visual impression that the stall is not clean. Large flake shavings have a very clean look and tend to smell nice for longer, but they may be a little tricky to pick through. You may end up feeling like you're wasting a lot when you use these shavings. Newer commercially available beddings, such as pellets and corn shavings, tend to be a little pricier, but they do a very good job at reducing ammonia smells. One word of caution about pellet bedding-- always read the directions. Some need to be watered down to activate them. Until they're activated, they're round and prone to rolling when walked upon by humans. I can't count the number of times I've slipped and fallen in a stall due to pellet bedding.

Straw is also commonly used as bedding, especially in breeding barns since it doesn't stick to newborn foals' skin or get inhaled into their delicate respiratory systems. Straw is very difficult to pick through and clean, which means you may simply need to remove absolutely everything from a stall bedded with straw. It also tends to take up a lot of room on the typical manure heap. It's definitely cheap and does its job well, but cleaning a stall bedded with straw is definitely more difficult than cleaning one filled with shavings.

As you truck along, you may discover that you have more questions than you have answers. This is very common and natural in the horse world. Thankfully, we live in an age where a quick search on your smartphone should provide you with enough information to deal with the immediate consequences of your question and point you in the direction of some helpful next steps or resources.

You may need a month or so to truly establish your routine with your horse. You may discover that the way you initially set up your barn isn't as conducive to your routine as you thought, too. There truly is a lot of trial and error in horse keeping. You will make mistakes along the way. You may forget to lock up the feed at night and discover a raccoon has helped himself to as much as he could. You will tip over a full wheelbarrow in the most inconvenient spot and spend twice as long cleaning it up. Your hay will go moldy at some point. Your water pipes will freeze. You will absolutely touch the electric fence at some point and regret it. It may seem like every day you find a new problem or challenge that must be dealt with that very second.

My advice for these situations is to breathe. Stay calm so you can think clearly in the moment. It is not your horse's fault that the wheelbarrow tipped-- unless your horse pawed at it or sent it sprawling with his nose. Whenever things happen, make sure your horse is secure first. Then allow yourself whatever emotional room you need at the moment.

Every horse person has enjoyed a bad day with some weird barn problem as the cherry on top. Cry on your horse's shoulder if you need to. Scream in the tack room if you need to. You'll likely find that your horse is far more sympathetic to your pain than you might imagine. Red is a very tall horse at 16.2 hands high. I have cried on his shoulder many times over our past eleven years together. He's a very good shoulder to cry on since it's perfectly placed for me to simply lean on him, but also because he doesn't like to see humans upset. He'll turn his head and sniff at me, gently bumping me with his nose. He stands perfectly still while I get out my sadness or frustration, and then, once I've pulled myself together, he'll rub his face on my back to make me laugh.

Over time, your routine will help you turn your barn chores into more of a barn privilege, and your horse will tend to agree that this is, in fact, the best life ever.

CONCLUSION

Now that you've discovered the basics of horse care, you might find yourself completely overwhelmed at how involved it can be. Not only are there a lot of moving parts, but it sounds like horses are difficult to keep alive. It sounds like long hours, heavy lifting, sweating, freezing, and a lot of money.

These assessments are true, but what in life doesn't require our blood, sweat, and tears? Car enthusiasts spend just as much time, money, and energy finding, repairing, and restoring their dream cars. Mountain climbers spend days, weeks, or months in preparation and risk their lives summiting the tallest peaks. Even the family dog requires frequent walks and potty breaks. Horses are not easy, but nothing in life truly is, especially if you love it completely.

It does take a very special kind of person to care for a horse. You have to be willing to smell strange and get dirty. You will find manure in your hair and on your face. You will need to look at some pretty gruesome wounds and ignore your disgust to take care of the oozing. You will get up earlier than you want and stay up later than you prefer. Your muscles will ache. You will miss out on some fun social activities. You may at some point "borrow" your horse's Epsom salts for your own soak.

But in return, you'll get the adoration and respect of a horse. Sure, your horse might not be as affectionate as Red, but remember-- this is a 1,000 pound beast who can run 25 miles per hour. He doesn't have to do a single thing you say unless he wants to. And over time, with proper care, he'll definitely want to. You'll hear that distinctive nicker when you come out to the barn to feed. You'll see his ears perk up when he hears your footsteps. He'll meet you at the barn door, ready to come in from turnout to spend some time with you.

Horses can't "talk" per se, in that they don't use human language to share their thoughts, but they are very honest in their actions. The deeper the bond you form with your horse, the more you'll know what's on their mind. Red, in particular, is one horse that is very clear about what he likes and doesn't like. He's tolerant of things that don't live up to his standards, but his antsy movement and caustic side-eye tell me exactly what I need to know about his opinions.

Making a horse happy will make you happy. Those quiet moments, when you're grooming your horse and suddenly hit the itchy spot, are the type that you'll cherish your entire life. You can tell all of your secrets to your horse. Your horse will listen to what a jerk your boss is, how your teachers don't understand you, or how your family is out of their minds, and he won't judge you for a single thing you say. Instead, he's more concerned that you give him water, food, medical care, and attention. And if you do all of that, and you're nice on top of that? You've made his life exponentially better.

As you've read, there's a lot to remember. I encourage everyone to come up with the reminders and resources they will need to help with each component of horse care. For example, I set a calendar reminder each week to pick up horse feed. I have supplements delivered to the barn automatically each month. I consult with my barn owner when it's time for the farrier to come out to take care of all their hooves, and I make sure I arrive on time when he comes out with cash in my hand to pay him for his services.

I personally recommend finding a mentor when starting out in horsekeeping. If you're boarding your horse, this may be your barn owner or trainer. Your 4-H equine advisor, or even a buddy you've exchanged messages with via an online forum, can provide lots of insight into common issues, or even direct you to the details you need. Horse people have a reputation for being a bit strange and overzealous, but reflecting back on the past several chapters, you may now understand why!

Over time, your daily horse care activities may become the highlight of your day. In a stressful world, it can be very enriching to take some time away from phones, computers, bosses, and email to just stand in the barn, listening to your horse quietly chomping on hay. After a hectic day of running errands and meeting deadlines, a quick, calm ride on your horse may be exactly what you need to unwind. In fact, there have been times when I simply pull a horse out of a stall and groom it from head to tail while working out some issue or complication in my non-horsey life.

Caring for a horse requires a level of discipline and dedication that you may not initially expect. People often ask me if it's "just like taking care of a giant baby," and while there are similarities, a horse is certainly more autonomous. A horse also isn't small enough to throw in a car seat or stroller for the day! When venturing into horse care, be prepared for plenty of sacrifices but appreciate the down time. Horses have instincts for a reason, and as long as you provide them with the food, water, and shelter they need, they'll be able to figure out quite a few things on their own. While domesticating an animal is a huge responsibility, it's important to remember that your horse doesn't actually need to be swaddled and tended to every minute of the day.

My hope is that this book has gotten you started on the path towards caring for your own horse. I certainly encourage you to check out the Resources section to continue researching any particular topic or area of care in which your horse may need some specialized attention. Don't consider this book the absolute encyclopedia of "Do's and Don'ts" of horsekeeping, but rather consider it more of a general text to set you on your course for learning all of the intricate details that will make your horse's particular experience much more enriching.

My wish is for you and your horse to have a long, fruitful, healthy relationship together. Whether you catch the "horse bug" and find yourself requiring at least one equine companion for the rest of your life, or only venture into horse ownership because you've found that one magical beast, I hope you enjoy the bond you form with your horse for many years to come. Yes, there will be good days and bad days, but at the end of each day, I hope that your heart will be filled with love and appreciation for that big, hairy, stinky manure machine that you've chosen to share your life with.

All the best, from my barn to yours.

Printed in Great Britain
by Amazon

46416625R00051